D0847729

*Beliefs, Attitudes,
and Values*

BELIEFS
ATTITUDES
AND
VALUES

A Theory of

Organization and Change

by Milton Rokeach

Jossey-Bass Inc., Publishers
615 Montgomery Street • San Francisco • 1968

LIBRARY — LUTHERAN SCHOOL
OF THEOLOGY AT CHICAGO

BF
773
.R6

BELIEFS, ATTITUDES, AND VALUES
A Theory of Organization and Change
by Milton Rokeach

Copyright © 1968 by Jossey-Bass, Inc., Publishers

Copyright under Pan American and Universal
Copyright Conventions

All rights reserved. No part of this book may
be reproduced in any form—except for brief
quotation in a review—without written
permission from the publisher. All inquiries
should be addressed to:

Jossey-Bass, Inc., Publishers
615 Montgomery Street
San Francisco, California 94111

Library of Congress Catalog Card Number 68-21322

Printed in the United States of America
by York Composition Company, Inc.
York, Pennsylvania

FIRST EDITION
68042

THE JOSSEY-BASS BEHAVIORAL SCIENCE SERIES

General Editors

WILLIAM E. HENRY, *University of Chicago*
NEVITT SANFORD, *Stanford University*

By MILTON ROKEACH

BELIEFS, ATTITUDES, AND VALUES

THE OPEN AND CLOSED MIND

THE THREE CHRISTS OF YPSILANTI

Preface

Beliefs, Attitudes, and Values represents a further elaboration of my continuing and perhaps single-minded interest in the nature of belief systems. The title reflects my view that an understanding of man's beliefs, attitudes, and values will not come about unless we are willing to distinguish these concepts from one another and to employ them in distinctively different ways; the subtitle conveys my view that beliefs, attitudes, and values are all organized together to form a functionally integrated cognitive system, so that a change in any part of the system will affect other parts, and will culminate in behavioral change.

Within the framework of a person-centered theory about the organization of belief systems I try herein to present a systematic and, I hope, a clear way of thinking about some of the problems that have not been satisfactorily handled in social psychology. There is as yet little consensus about exactly what we mean when we speak of a belief, an attitude, a value, a value system—and exactly what the differences are among these concepts. We sometimes employ these and similar concepts in the singular and sometimes in the plural, as if we have not yet learned how to count them; and we tend to employ them arbitrarily and interchangeably, thus leading us into what Donald T. Campbell has aptly called a "terminological forest." We have few conceptual guidelines for assessing the extent to which a given belief or attitude is important or unimportant. We are still a long way from understanding the theoretical relationship between attitudes and behavior, between attitude change and behavioral change, and we have not yet learned how to predict accurately one from the other. The great majority of experimental findings on attitude change, I argue, have little to do with attitude change, since the findings can be more simply accounted for on other grounds. The attitude change literature does not seem to serve the interests of the educator and therapist nearly so much as it serves the interests of specialized persuaders in advertising, the mass media, politics, and public relations.

I have noticed that social scientists from other disciplines, philosophers, and theologians are quickly bored by accounts of research on attitudes but perk up when the discussion is broadened to include beliefs and values. The same is true of the undergraduate and graduate students in my social psychology courses. By extending the scope of my treatment to include beliefs and values as well as attitudes I am departing from the traditional overemphasis on attitudes typically found in contemporary social psychology textbooks and books of readings. I therefore hope that this book will be useful not only to my colleagues, but also to students in social psychology as well as those in sociology, philosophy, anthropology, political science, education, social work, and theology.

I have brought together here a number of my papers written over the past five years on beliefs, attitudes, and values. Except for Chapter Two, all of these papers were previously published and it is gratifying to see them combined under one cover. They belong together. The ideas presented in any one chapter actually developed out of those in the chapters preceding it.

Chapter One discusses five types of belief we all possess, ordered along a central-peripheral dimension, and it presents several conceptual criteria for assessing order of importance of belief. Several hypotheses are derived about the relative resistance to change of beliefs, varying in importance and about the consequences expected to follow from such change. This is followed by empirical observations that are in one way or another considered relevant to these hypotheses.

Chapter Two, coauthored with Joseph Reyher and Richard Wiseman, presents for the first time a full report on the results of an experiment on the hypnotic induction of change in belief systems. This research is the experimental and more rigorous counterpart of my earlier and more clinically oriented study of *The Three Christs of Ypsilanti*. Fifty-five beliefs varying in centrality were systematically altered by hypnotic suggestion over a period of several weeks and their effects were measured.

Chapter Three is a slightly modified version of a paper previously published, in collaboration with my student Louis Mezei, in *Science*. It presents the results of real-life experiments wherein similarity of belief was pitted against similarity of race to ascertain which is the more important determinant of interpersonal attraction and choice. In lectures to professional psychologists and sociologists, and to student and adult groups, I have often invited my audience to guess the obtained results on the importance of race as a determinant of choice from their own theories of race relations. The obtained data are provocative and dissonance-producing if for no other reason than that they fall outside the range of results predicted by professionals and laymen alike.

Chapter Four is a somewhat modified version of a paper previously published, in collaboration with my student Gilbert Rothman, in the *Psychological Review*. The principle of belief congruence is extended into a more generalized model of cognitive interaction, differing in several important respects from Osgood and Tannenbaum's congruity principle. Data are presented to assess the relative validity of the two models.

Chapter Five is a more extended version of my paper on the nature of attitudes, recently published in the *International Encyclopedia of the Social Sciences*. I have taken some pains in this chapter to state in what ways beliefs differ from attitudes and, more important, to state explicitly in what ways my own formulations about the nature of attitudes are similar to and different from traditional formulations. A major idea that I put forward and develop is that behavior cannot be determined by one attitude alone, that a minimum of two attitudes are necessary to activate behavior. I have also tried to bring up to date Allport's classic article on attitudes, written over thirty years ago.

The two-attitude theory of behavior presented in Chapter Five is extended in Chapter Six to consider its implications for theory and research on attitude change and behavioral change. I then suggest some needed improvements in the design of attitude change experiments, which I illustrate with various examples.

In Chapter Seven, first presented as a presidential address to the Society for the Psychological Study of Social Issues, I suggest that the time is now perhaps ripe to shift social psychology's main focus away from theory and experiment on attitude organization and change to value organization and change. This, of course, implies that a clear-cut conceptual distinction between attitude and value is possible, and I attempt it here. I then try to develop a theory about the manner in which attitudes and values are cognitively organized; this theory provides a framework for comparing various balance theories with one another, as well as a framework for further research on conditions that might lead to enduring value and attitude change. Some data are then presented that tentatively suggest that enduring changes in important values and attitudes are possible as a result of establishing certain education- rather than persuasion-oriented experimental procedures.

Finally, I have included in Appendices A and B two applied papers, one concerned with advertising and the other with religion.

In the first paper I propose that Madison Avenue's special predicament arises from the particular type of belief it specializes in trying to change. In the second paper I propose that institutionalized religion's special predicament arises from a conflict between the contradictory beliefs it unwittingly inculcates in its adherents. In both of these papers I make use of concepts presented in the main part of this book.

The work reported here was supported primarily by the National Science Foundation and secondarily by the School of Labor and Industrial Relations at Michigan State University. I am extremely grateful to both organizations for past and continuing financial support.

I want to thank William E. Henry and Nevitt Sanford, general editors for Jossey-Bass Publishers; their enthusiastic reception of my work encouraged me to bring out this book. I want to express deep appreciation to Judy Hale, my secretary, for the many ways in which she relieved me from burdensome details and for her indispensable help in preparing this manuscript for publication.

MILTON ROKEACH

East Lansing, Michigan
March, 1968

Contents

Beliefs, Attitudes,
and Values

ONE

The Organization and Modification of Beliefs

Nearly everyone would agree that the total number of beliefs a grown person possesses is large. By the time we have reached adulthood we have formed tens, possibly thousands of beliefs concerning what is or is not true and beautiful and good about the physical and social world in which we live.

It is inconceivable that these countless beliefs would be retained in an unorganized, chaotic state within our minds. Rather, it must be assumed that man's beliefs—like the physicist's electrons and protons, like the astronomer's moons and planets and suns, like the geneticist's chromosomes and genes—become somehow organized into architectural systems having describable and measurable structural properties which, in turn, have observable behavioral consequences.

1

When I use the term belief I am not necessarily referring to verbal reports taken at face value; beliefs are inferences made by an observer about underlying states of expectancy. When a person says: "This I believe . . . ," he may or may not be representing accurately what he truly believes because there are often compelling personal and social reasons, conscious and unconscious, why he will not or cannot tell us. For these reasons beliefs—like motives, genes, and neutrons—cannot be directly observed but must be inferred as best one can, with whatever psychological devices available, from all the things the believer says or does.

A belief system may be defined as having represented within it, in some organized psychological but not necessarily logical form, each and every one of a person's countless beliefs about physical and social reality. By definition, we do not allow beliefs to exist outside the belief system for the same reason that the astronomer does not allow stars to remain outside the universe.

There are at least seven major interrelated questions that it is possible to ask about the nature of man's systems of belief. First, what structural properties do all belief systems have in common, regardless of content? Second, in what structural ways do belief systems differ from one another? Third, how are they developed and learned? Fourth, what motivational functions do belief systems serve? Fifth, what is the relation between belief and emotion or, in other terms, between cognition and affection? Sixth, how do belief systems guide perceiving, thinking, remembering, learning, and acting? And, finally, what conditions facilitate or hinder the modification of belief systems?

It is not my intent to discuss all these questions here; they are mentioned only to point to the broader theoretical framework for the present concern, which is to focus particular attention on theory, method, and findings relevant to the first and last of the seven questions mentioned, those concerned with the organization and modification of systems of belief. It is my hope that the discussion will increase understanding of a variety of situations in real life in which man's belief systems seem to undergo change. For example, changes in systems of beliefs are often said to occur following successful therapy or political or religious conversion, or, conversely, following ideological disillusionment and defection. Mention might be made also of various coercive attempts to alter belief systems, such as the "thought reform" procedures employed in Communist China and the so-called "brainwashing" techniques employed in North Korean prisoner-of-war camps and, somewhat earlier, by Khrushchev's own admission, in the great Soviet purge trials of the mid-Thirties.

ANALYSIS OF TYPES OF BELIEFS

I begin the analysis with three simple assumptions. First, not all beliefs are equally important to the individual; beliefs vary along a central-peripheral dimension. Second, the more central a belief, the more it will resist change. Third, the more central the belief changed, the more widespread the repercussions in the rest of the belief system. These assumptions are not unlike the assumptions made by the atomic physicist who conceives of a central nucleus within the atom wherein the particles within the nucleus are held together in a stable structure, and contain vast amounts of potential energy. Under some circumstances, for example, through processes of fission or fusion, the potential energy contained within the nucleus will be released, thus changing the structure of the nucleus and, thereby, the structure of the whole atom. Is it possible, in a roughly analogous fashion, to conceive of belief systems as having "nuclear" beliefs? And would an understanding of their nature and how to alter that nature lead us to understand better why belief systems are typically in a relatively stable state highly resistant to change, and under what conditions they will change?

By what logical criteria can one decide which ones of a person's countless beliefs are central or important and which ones are less so? Obviously all these beliefs do not play an equally prominent role within a person's belief system; nor do they play an equally prominent role in determining his behavior. The assessment of importance is a question with which many students of social attitude have concerned themselves. Thus, Katz (1944, p. 51) writes: "The

3

problem of the depth of opinion, or the intensity of belief, is perhaps one of the most basic questions in the measurement of public opinion." Krech and Crutchfield (1948, p. 251) apparently share Katz's view: "The degree to which an attitude is important or central to the individual is one of the most critical attributes requiring measurement." And Pepitone (1966, p. 267), in a critical review of contemporary consistency models, points out that they "either do not deal with the problem of importance at all or deal with it inadequately."

One may be concerned with variations in the importance of a particular belief among different persons or with variations in the importance of several beliefs within a single person's belief system. It is possible in either case to measure importance by strictly empirical means, such as rating (Rosenberg, 1960), ranking, or paired comparison (Rokeach and Rothman, 1965) methods; or beliefs may be classified *a priori* as varying in importance on the basis of one or more conceptual criteria and may then be empirically validated.

A conceptual approach to variations in the importance of a given belief (or opinion or attitude) across persons and groups is perhaps best exemplified in the work of Sherif and associates (1965). They conceptually define variations in an attitude's importance in terms of the concept of ego-involvement, and assume that variations in ego-involvement with a specific issue are overtly manifested by latitude of rejection, or by membership or nonmembership in a social group committed to a given issue. Eagly (1967), defining a given attitude's centrality in terms of the number of other concepts dependent on it, assumes that an attitude that concerns the self-concept is more central than an attitude that does not concern the self-concept. Rosenberg (1960) defines the importance of a given attitude as depending on the extent to which it is perceived to be instrumental to the furtherance or hindrance of important values, but importance of values is empirically determined.

Our main concern here is with the development of a conceptual approach to the relative importance or centrality of various types of beliefs within a given belief system. We first propose and elaborate on a major defining attribute of importance and then identify five classes of beliefs within the belief system that can be ordered by this attribute along a central-peripheral dimension. From this formulation we derive several hypotheses concerning differential resistance to change of beliefs varying in centrality, and the effects of such differential change on the rest of the belief system.

We define importance solely in terms of connectedness: the more a given belief is functionally connected or in communication with other beliefs, the more implications and consequences it has for other beliefs and, therefore, the more central the belief. This definition, however, requires further elaboration if it is to be useful. What sorts of beliefs can reasonably be assumed to be relatively high in functional connectedness or in functional communication with other beliefs? We propose the following four defining assumptions or criteria of connectedness:

1. *Existential versus nonexistential beliefs.* Beliefs directly concerning one's own existence and identity in the physical and social world are assumed to have more functional connections and consequences for other beliefs than those which less directly concern one's existence and identity.

2. *Shared versus unshared beliefs about existence and self-identity.* Beliefs concerning existence and self-identity may be shared or not shared with others. Those shared with others are assumed to have more functional connections and consequences for other beliefs than those not shared with others.

3. *Derived versus underived beliefs.* Many beliefs are learned not by direct encounter with the object of belief but, indirectly, from reference persons and groups. We refer to such beliefs as "derived" beliefs. Derived beliefs are assumed to have fewer functional connections and consequences for other beliefs than the beliefs from which they are derived.

4. *Beliefs concerning and not concerning matters of taste.* Many beliefs represent more or less arbitrary matters of taste and are often so perceived by the individual holding

5

them. Such beliefs are assumed to have relatively fewer functional connections and consequences for other beliefs than beliefs that do not represent arbitrary matters of taste.

We comment further on these four defining assumptions of connectedness as we next describe five classes of beliefs within the belief system thus far identified. We conceive these beliefs to be arranged as follows along a central-peripheral dimension.

TYPE A: PRIMITIVE BELIEFS, 100 PER CENT CONSENSUS

Most central are those beliefs that are learned by direct encounter with the object of belief (that is, they are not derived from other beliefs) and that are, moreover, reinforced by a unanimous social consensus among all of one's reference persons and groups. Type A beliefs are psychologically incontrovertible because they are rarely, if ever, experienced as subjects of controversy and therefore have an axiomatic, taken-for-granted character. It is as if the believer says to himself: "I believe, and everyone else who could know believes it too."

Such primitive beliefs can be thought of as being represented within the innermost core of the belief system. They are called "primitive" because they are roughly analogous to the primitive terms of an axiomatic system in mathematics or science. A person's primitive beliefs represent his "basic truths" about physical reality, social reality, and the nature of the self; they represent a subsystem within the total system in which the person has the heaviest of commitments. In the ordinary course of life's events, they are so much taken for granted that they do not come up as a subject for discussion or controversy. "I believe this is a table," "I believe this is my mother," "I believe my name is so-and-so" are examples, respectively, of primitive beliefs about the physical world, the social world, and the self—supported by a unanimous consensus among those in a position to know.

Another way of describing primitive beliefs about physical reality, the social world, and the self is to talk about *object constancy, person constancy,* and *self-constancy.* Even though I see this rectangular table from many angles, I continue to believe (primitively) that it remains a table and that it remains rectangular. What many perception psychologists have overlooked thus far is that object constancy is also a social phenomenon, built up in childhood side-by-side with person constancy, both object and person constancy being necessary prerequisites for developing a sense of self-constancy. Not only does a child learn that objects maintain their constancy, but also that other people constantly experience physical objects as he does. Thus, two subsets of Type A beliefs are built up together, one about the constancy of physical objects and the other about the constancy of people with respect to physical objects.

Object constancy and person constancy seem to serve important functions for the growing child. They build up within him a basic minimum of *trust* that the physical world will stay put and also that the world of people can be depended on to react constantly to physical objects as he does. It is as if nature and society had conspired to provide the child with a minimum guarantee of stability on which to build his own sense of self-constancy. Actually, the child seems to need and to strive for far more person constancy than that provided by the physical contexts within which he learns object constancy. A child depends on his mother to remain his mother (with all that is meant by mother), and on his family and social groups to remain his family and social groups, no less than on a table to remain a table.

It may be supposed that any inexplicable disruption of these taken-for-granted constancies, physical or social or self, would lead one to question the validity of one's own senses, one's competence as a person who can cope with reality, or even one's sanity. Put another way, violation of any primitive beliefs supported by unanimous consensus may lead to serious disruption of beliefs about self-constancy or self-identity, and from this disruption other disturbances should follow, for example, disturbances in one's feelings of competence and effectance (White, 1959); it would lead one to question the validity of many other beliefs within one's belief system; it would produce a great deal of inconsistency within the belief system, that, to eliminate, would require major cognitive reorganization in the

7

content and in the structural relations among many other beliefs within the system.

In the beginning all beliefs are probably primitive ones, since the young child is not yet capable of understanding that some beliefs are not shared by everybody. The young child's mental capacities and experience are too circumscribed for him to grasp the fact that he lives in a world in which there is controversy, or even armed conflict, over which authorities are positive and which are negative, and which beliefs and ideologies associated with authority are the most valid. In the very beginning there is only one authority the infant looks to for information and nurturance—the mother; somewhat later, the father. These parental referents are the only referents that exist for the young child; he does not yet know that there are other positive referents, or that negative referents exist.

As the infant develops toward maturity, many of his primitive beliefs will continue to remain primitive, providing they do not arise as subjects of controversy. As the child grows and broadens the range of his interactions to include others outside the family, his authority base becomes gradually extended to include virtually everyone in a position to know. Thus, should any doubt arise about the validity of such a primitive belief—for example, is today Wednesday or Thursday?—he can check it by asking virtually any stranger who happens along.

TYPE B: PRIMITIVE BELIEFS, ZERO CONSENSUS

Not all primitive beliefs owe their primitiveness to the universalization of social consensus. A second type of incontrovertible belief directly involving existence and self-identity is also learned by direct encounter with the object of belief, but its maintenance does not seem to depend on its being shared with others: there are no reference persons or groups outside the self who could controvert such a belief. Through adverse experience, some primitive beliefs may be formed in which support from external authority is abandoned altogether. Beliefs that are not shared with others are therefore impervious to persuasion or argument by others. Even though such beliefs may sometimes become a subject of controversy, they are psychologically incontrovertible. For example, a child may come to believe through intense experience or through an accretion of less intense experiences that he lives in a totally hostile world, or that he is unlovable, or, phobically, that certain heretofore benign objects or places are now dangerous. In this second kind of primitive belief, it is as if the believer says: "I believe, but no one else could know. It therefore does not matter what others believe." Or, to quote from a more popular refrain: "Nobody knows the troubles I've seen." Examples of such beliefs are those held on pure faith—phobias, delusions, hallucinations, and various ego-enhancing and ego-deflating beliefs arising from learned experience (for example, *No matter what others believe,* I believe in God, I believe I am a reasonably intelligent person, I believe I am a stupid person, I believe my mother does not love me, I believe my son is a good boy).

TYPE C: AUTHORITY BELIEFS

As the child interacts with others, his expanding repertoire of primitive beliefs is continually brought into play and he thus stands to discover at any moment that a particular belief he had heretofore believed everyone else believed, such as the belief in God or Country or Santa Claus, is not shared by everyone. At this point the child is forced to work through a more selective conception of positive and negative authority; this point marks the beginning of the development of the nonprimitive parts of the child's ever-expanding belief system.

Nonprimitive beliefs are conceived to develop out of Type A beliefs and to be in a functional relationship with them. They seem to serve the purpose of helping the person to round out his picture of the world, realistically and rationally to the extent possible, defensively and irrationally to the extent necessary. In using the concept of nonprimitive beliefs, I am trying to point to a class of beliefs that do not seem to have the same taken-for-granted character as Type A primitive beliefs. We learn to expect differences of opinion and controversy concerning them, however much we might cherish

9

them. Such beliefs, while important and generally resistant to change, are nevertheless conjectured to be less important and easier to change than Types A and B beliefs.

Most important of these nonprimitive beliefs seem to be those concerning positive and negative authority—what the sociologists call reference persons or reference groups. Such beliefs concern not only which authorities *could* know but also which authorities *would* know. Which authorities, positive and negative, are we to trust and distrust, to look to and not look to, as we go about our daily lives seeking information about the world? The particular authorities relied on for information differ from one person to the next and would depend on learning experiences within the context of the person's social structure—family, class, peer group, ethnic group, religious and political groups, and country.

At first only the child's parents serve as reference persons, and beliefs about other referents are derived from parents. But as the child grows his range of positive and negative reference persons and groups becomes gradually extended through direct encounter (for example, country, teacher, peer). Any given authority belief is typically controvertible because the believer has learned that some of his reference persons and groups do and some do not share his belief.

TYPE D: DERIVED BELIEFS

Believing in the credibility of a particular authority implies an acceptance of other beliefs perceived to emanate from such authority. Such beliefs are defined as "derived" beliefs, and are controvertible for the same reason Type C beliefs are controvertible. Ideological beliefs originating with religious or political institutions, and derived secondhand through processes of identification with authority rather than by direct encounter with the object of belief, are assumed to be Type D beliefs. Beliefs concerning matters of fact that are held solely because we trust an authoritative source (for example, *Encyclopaedia Britannica, New York Times,* a history book) are also assumed to represent Type D beliefs.

If we know that a person believes in a particular authority, we should be able to deduce many of his other beliefs, those which emanate or derive from the authorities he identifies with. Such derived beliefs are less important dynamically than beliefs about authority, and therefore a change of belief with respect to authority, or a direct communication from one's authority, should lead to many other changes in beliefs deriving from authority. These derived beliefs form what is ordinarily referred to as an institutionalized ideology and, along with the identifications with reference persons and groups on which such ideologies are based, provide one with a sense of group identity.

TYPE E: INCONSEQUENTIAL BELIEFS

Many beliefs within the belief system seem to represent more or less arbitrary matters of taste, and we shall henceforth call such beliefs "inconsequential" beliefs. Like Types A and B beliefs, they are incontrovertible because they originate in direct experience with the object of belief and their maintenance does not necessarily require social consensus. This is consistent with the oft-heard cliché: "There is no arguing over matters of taste." Like other beliefs, they may be intensely held. Matters of taste are, nevertheless, considered to be inconsequential because they have few or no connections with other beliefs. If changed, they have few or no implications or consequences for maintaining other beliefs involving self-identity and self-esteem, or for requiring consistency-restoring reorganization within the rest of the system.

In summary, a person's total belief system includes inconsequential beliefs, derived beliefs, pre-ideological beliefs about specific authority, and pre-ideological primitive beliefs, socially shared or unshared, about the nature of the physical world, society, and the self. All such beliefs are assumed to be formed and developed very early in the life of a child. They are undoubtedly first learned in the context of interactions with parents. As the child grows older, he learns that there are certain beliefs that virtually all others believe, other beliefs that are true for him even though no one else believes them, other important beliefs about which men differ, and other beliefs that are arbitrary matters of taste. Taken together, the total belief system may be seen as an organization of beliefs varying in depth, formed as a result of living in nature and in society, designed to help a person maintain, insofar as possible, a sense of ego and group identity, stable and continuous over time—an identity that is a part of, and simultaneously apart from, a stable physical and social environment.

Given these five types of beliefs to be ordered along a central-peripheral dimension, 120 different orders are possible. The particular way we have ordered the five types of belief is not only intuitively self-evident but can also be logically derived from the four defining criteria of connectedness mentioned earlier:[1]

1. Type E beliefs are less central than Types A, B, C, and D beliefs because the former have fewer connections with other beliefs (Assumption 4).

2. Type D beliefs are less central than Type C beliefs because the former are derived from the latter (Assumption 3).

3. Types C and D beliefs are less central than Types A and B because the latter directly concern beliefs about the self while the former do not (Assumption 1).

4. Finally, Type B beliefs are less central than Type A beliefs because the former do not depend on social consensus while the latter are unanimously shared with all of one's reference persons and groups (Assumption 2).

It will be noted that we have not relied on the criterion of

[1] While the specific ordering of the five beliefs was not derived from any particular personality theory, the ordering is probably also compatible, in whole or part, with most theories of personality development, especially psychoanalytic theory, which implicitly assumes that importance of belief is a function of ontogenesis. Type A beliefs would correspond to what Fenichel (1945, pp. 35–36) has described as the earliest stage of development of a "sense of reality" and "body image"; Type B beliefs would correspond to beliefs concerning one's own drives, emotions, and self-esteem; Type C beliefs would correspond to "superego" beliefs or to internalized representations of society; Type D beliefs would correspond to various cognitive derivatives of identification with authority. As for Type E beliefs, it would be difficult to translate them into psychoanalytic terms since every belief, however trivial or inconsequential, is assumed by psychoanalysis to be psychodynamically meaningful and consequential.

12

intensity to order the five types of beliefs. They can be ordered along a central-peripheral dimension even though they are all equated for intensity. While there is undoubtedly a positive correlation between centrality and intensity, the relationship is by no means a necessary one. Many inconsequential or trivial beliefs (Type E) can be intensely held and strongly defended. One may, for example, intensely believe that rare steaks are tastier than well-done steaks, or that more enjoyable vacations await us at the seashore than in the mountains. Such beliefs are nevertheless inconsequential because they have relatively few connections with, and if changed, have relatively few consequences for, other beliefs.

But intensity becomes a more compelling criterion of importance as we move away from a consideration of the relative importance of beliefs between classes to a consideration of beliefs within each class. While it is not possible to specify in advance on conceptual grounds which beliefs within a class will be more or less intense, it is possible to order such beliefs empirically along an intensity dimension. In the research to be described in Chapter Two, however, we hold intensity constant since we are primarily interested in the effects of constant pressures to change beliefs across rather than within classes.

Another defining attribute sometimes mentioned in the literature as a criterion of importance is verifiability of belief. There are, however, grounds for doubting that verifiable beliefs are necessarily more central than unverifiable beliefs. To be sure, Type A beliefs, which are verifiable, are more central than Type B beliefs, which are unverifiable. But Type B beliefs, which include unverifiable beliefs based on faith, delusion, and hallucination, are more central than many verifiable Type D beliefs. We may, for example, believe that Jupiter has twelve moons not because we have seen them with our own eyes but because we believe a trusted authoritative source. Such beliefs, while verifiable, are, nonetheless, considered to be derived beliefs (in the present conception, Type D beliefs) that can probably be easily changed by a persuasive message from a trusted source.

13

SOME EMPIRICAL FINDINGS

To be discussed next are several early studies designed to test various hypotheses stemming from our formulations about the central-peripheral dimension. In our first study, carried out in collaboration with Albert Zavala, we tried to ascertain the perceived resistance to change, perceived social consensus, and intensity of beliefs varying in centrality. In this study we employed three types of beliefs—Types A, C, and D—rather than all five types presented here. (Type B beliefs were excluded because they were not suitable for investigation by group questionnaire methodology; Type E beliefs—inconsequential beliefs—were excluded because they had not yet been formulated.)

Table 1 shows nine statements that were presented to about 70 subjects representing the three kinds of beliefs—Types A, C, and D. The subjects were asked to rank these nine statements in terms of which one they would be most reluctant to relinquish under any circumstance, which one they would be next most reluctant to relinquish, and so on. The subjects were also asked to indicate how strongly they agreed with each of the nine beliefs and to estimate how many others believed as they did with respect to each of the nine beliefs.

The first column of Table 1 shows the rank order of resistance to change of the nine beliefs, as judged by our subjects. It is seen that the three primitive ones are ranked highest in resistance to change. These are followed by the three authority beliefs and, finally, by the three derived beliefs. The rankings of all nine beliefs conform to theoretical expectations without exception. Moreover, as shown in the second column of Table 1, the vast majority of our subjects adhere to Type A beliefs with absolute intensity while considerably fewer subjects do so with respect to authority and derived beliefs. Finally, as shown in the last column of Table 1, about three-fourths of our subjects report that all others unanimously believe as they do with respect to primitive beliefs while only a scattered few claim unanimous social consensus for authority and derived beliefs. Thus, the theoretical distinctions drawn among these three types of beliefs

14

Table 1

Degree of Resistance to Change, Intensity of Agreement, and Perceived Consensus of Type A, C, and D Beliefs

	MEAN RANK	PER CENT WHO ABSOLUTELY ACCEPT OR REJECT BELIEF	PER CENT REPORTING UNANIMOUS SOCIAL CONSENSUS
Type A (primitive)			
1. Death is inevitable.	2.47	92	72
2. We cannot live unless we have oxygen.	2.67	91	74
3. My name is.................................	2.86	98	83
Mean		93.7	76.3
Type C (authority)			
4. There is only one true Bible.	4.17	50	4
5. The U. S. Constitution is the best constitution ever framed.	5.30	21	7
6. The Pope is infallible in matters of faith and morals.	5.97	55	2
Mean		42.0	4.3
Type D (derived)			
7. I favor birth control.	6.37	48	2
8. Adam had a navel.	7.22	28	9
9. It is wrong to smoke.	7.89	34	0
Mean		36.7	3.7

are operationally demonstrated. Naïve subjects who know nothing of our theory seem to behave as if they, too, can tell the difference among the three kinds of beliefs.

These results suggest that beliefs about such things as the Bible, the fallibility or infallibility of the Pope, or the United States

Constitution are not among the most deeply held of man's beliefs. More deeply held and possibly more resistant to change are those beliefs that all men would share with one another and that rarely come up for discussion or controversy, namely, Type A beliefs. These results suggest further that in the event of a conflict between two beliefs varying in centrality, the more central belief would win out. Such a conflict is neatly exemplified in a slogan we are all familiar with, a political slogan first made famous by Bertrand Russell, "Better red than dead," and the counterslogan "Better dead than red." These slogans are theoretically interesting because they pit two beliefs against each other, one a primitive, existential belief that is shared by everybody, "It is better to be alive than dead," and the other an ideological belief—in our terms, a derived belief—"It is better to be anti-Communist than Communist." In line with our theory, we would have to predict that most people, even anti-Communist Americans, would prefer the state of redness to the state of deadness, simply because of the greater potency of primitive, existential beliefs over derived beliefs.

To find out if this is indeed so, a study was conducted in 1963 at Michigan State University in collaboration with Irwin Horowitz in which subjects were simply asked to agree or disagree with the statement: "Death is preferable to living under a Communist regime." Only 40 per cent reported that they would rather be dead than red, while 60 per cent reported they would rather be red than dead. But the finding of 40 per cent who prefer being dead seems questionable in the light of additional data. We found further that a majority of the better-dead-than-red group believed that no one would be mad enough to start a nuclear holocaust, and a majority of them did not believe that war is probable in the next decade. Since the subjects were college students, it may be assumed that a decade represents a very long time for them. In other words, the subjects who said they prefer death to life under Communism did not seem to conceive of their own death as a realistic or immediate possibility: they would rather be dead than red, but no one would be mad enough to start a nuclear war; and, besides, it would not come within the next decade. In contrast, a sizable majority of the better-

16

red-than-dead group admitted to the fear that a madman could start an atomic war at any moment. On the basis of these additional data, it may be doubted that even 40 per cent of our sample really prefer death to life under Communism.

Following a similar line of reasoning, it may be suggested that whenever people have been given a choice between such alternatives as death or life under fascism, between death or religious conversion, as was the case during the Spanish Inquisition, their belief and need systems were so constituted that, by and large, they preferred life to death. Thus on psychological grounds, I would not be inclined to accept seriously an invitation to die for this or that cause because it is doubtful that those who advocate dying for causes would, when the chips are down, themselves die for that cause. The deliberate choice of death over life for some cause is probably an extremely rare event in human history, and martyrdom is probably better understood as a state conferred *a posteriori* rather than freely chosen *a priori*.

All the preceding is not to deny, of course, that most of us possess primitive beliefs regarding conditions under which we would prefer death to life. For example, most mothers primitively believe that they would sacrifice their own lives to save the life of a loved child. Most of us primitively believe that we would prefer to die rather than betray a comrade to death at the hands of an enemy. But such instances are altogether different from those previously discussed. What seems to be involved in the examples just cited is not a primitive belief pitted against a peripheral belief but two or more primitive beliefs supported by unanimous social consensus, or altogether independent of social consensus, about the value of the life of one's own child as compared with one's own, or about the utter worthlessness of one's own life when bought at the expense of a comrade's.

What happens emotionally and cognitively when primitive beliefs are suddenly and inexplicably disrupted by strong external pressure? We have observed that if a parent suddenly calls his child by a name other than his own, the child will at first enjoy it, thinking it a new game. The child will encourage the parent to continue this game but will soon become apprehensive and ask for the parent's reassurance that it is only a game. If the reassurance is not forthcoming, the child will invariably develop a strong anxiety reaction within a matter of minutes and will engage in desperate efforts to get his parent to terminate the game. Apparently the strong panic reaction is a result of the violation of the child's primitive belief in his own identity, a belief the child learned in the first place from his parent, who is certainly in a position to know the child's name.

When the name-change experiment is repeated in a nursery school situation with an adult stranger rather than a parent, no anxiety reactions are observed. The child is easily able to defend himself against the attempt to violate his primitive belief in identity by responding that the stranger, because he is a stranger, is in no position to know his name. The preschool child typically responds: "You don't know who I am because you don't know my mother."

Beliefs about self-identity are not the only primitive beliefs which, if disrupted by those in a position to know, lead to strong emotional disturbance. Similar reactions can be observed when a child's primitive belief in the identity of his mother is suddenly and effectively challenged by the mother herself when she playfully pretends she is someone else or pretends she is some animal, yet refuses to reassure the child that she is merely pretending. One typically observes, as a result, sudden outbreaks of tears and other symptoms of the anxiety reaction.

Consider next several instances in which there are violations of primitive beliefs about physical reality. The television program *Candid Camera* often achieves its "entertaining" effects precisely because the audience is observing the reactions of persons whose primitive beliefs are being violated. Another example comes from the well-known Asch experiments (1952), in which a subject overhears five other subjects in a group experiment report that two lines are of equal length when in fact they are clearly of unequal length. The subject does not know that these other five subjects are really confederates of the experimenter, instructed in advance to give the same wrong answer when comparing lines of varying length. This experiment is typically emotionally upsetting to the subject because all the other subjects are clearly in a position to know, yet they all disagree with him. There has been a violation of primitive belief that is relieved only when, at the end, the subject is let in on the nature of the experiment.

The Asch experiment on judgment of line length, the *Candid Camera* effects, and the situations described involving a change of name all seem to have something in common. In all cases, a primitive, existential belief has been violated resulting in a strong anxiety reaction, which is relieved by reassurance: it was only an experiment; it was only a game; "Smile, you're on *Candid Camera.*" In all cases the experience is short-lived and terminated well before severe emotional disturbances set in. It is frightening to speculate what would have happened if such experiences had been prolonged. For example, what would be the outcome for a child if the change-of-name game were played for, say, a whole week? One can only speculate about the possible consequences—loss of identity, a breakdown of belief systems, and, in the extreme, a schizophrenic shattering of personality.

We can obtain at least a hint of what might happen under such prolonged experiences by considering the recent reports on "thought reform," "brainwashing," and voluntary confession (Lifton, 1961; Shein, 1956). It would seem from such reports that under such conditions as isolation, absolute control of information from the outside world, and the removal of the usual group supports, there is a loss of ego and group identity, and with the substitution of new group supports, the way is paved for the emergence of new identities, changes in ideology, voluntary confession, and collaboration. But it is difficult to determine the exact conditions that led to changes in some prisoners and not in others, and to gauge the exact changes in belief produced in those who did change. Physical hardship and duress were often present, and the methods of control varied from time to time, from prison to prison, and from prisoner to prisoner. Differences in the personality, status, and education of the prisoners were also unknown variables.

Ethical considerations clearly forbid social scientists from

19

conducting "thought control" experiments or tampering with a normal child's or adult's primitive beliefs for prolonged periods. Because of such considerations it was necessary to turn away from further investigations with normal persons to focus instead on psychotic persons holding delusional belief systems. The object of psychotherapy and social policy is to alter the psychotic's delusional beliefs and to readjust him to reality insofar as possible. Thus, experimental attempts over prolonged periods to change beliefs become ethically more justifiable when they serve therapeutic rather than destructive or "thought control" or "brainwashing" ends.

Such considerations led me to bring together for study over a two-year period three chronic paranoid schizophrenic patients, each believing he was the reincarnation of Jesus Christ. Leon, in his mid-thirties, had been hospitalized five years before. Joseph was in his late fifties and Clyde was about seventy years of age. The latter two had been institutionalized almost two decades before. The three delusional Christs were assigned to adjacent beds in one ward, ate at one table in the dining room, worked together on the same job, and met daily for group discussions. Each one was thus confronted with two others laying claim to the same identity within a controlled environment for a prolonged period. In addition, other experimental procedures were employed with Leon and Joseph. They received written suggestions to change their beliefs and behavior from authority figures they looked up to, figures who existed only in their imagination. Actually these communications were written and sent by me. All such procedures were designed to test the following hypotheses. First, having to live with others claiming the same identity over a prolonged period is as dissonance-producing a situation as is humanly conceivable and, consequently, changes in delusional beliefs and in behavior designed to reduce this dissonance should result. Second, a persuasive communication emanating from one's positive authority figure can only be responded to in one of two ways: either the suggestion to change is accepted from the positive authority or, if it is unacceptable, the attitude toward the positive authority figure will undergo change. In either event, changes in delusions should result.

The full story of what happened as a result of these experimental procedures is reported in *The Three Christs of Ypsilanti* (Rokeach, 1964). At the risk of oversimplification, let me here try to summarize briefly the main findings. First, the effect of confrontations over identity produced changes in the identity and delusional beliefs of the youngest of the three delusional Christs, the changes involving the destruction of existing delusions and the formation of new delusions concerning identity, bolstered by additional delusions emerging for the first time. Second, the persuasive communications from delusional authority figures produced many changes in the delusions and behavior of Leon and Joseph, including eventually the destruction of both Leon's and Joseph's delusional authority figures. In general, Leon, the youngest of the three, changed most as a result of our experimental procedures and Clyde, the oldest, changed the least.

It should be emphasized that although each of our investigations has served to increase our understanding of the internal architecture of belief systems and of the conditions for their modification, we have not yet learned how to control experimentally induced modifications in belief systems in order to achieve socially desirable therapeutic effects. In the last experiment referred to, we were indeed able to produce changes but we were not able to control the direction the changes took. It would thus seem that the nuclear physicists are far ahead of us in this respect; they have not only learned how to produce a schizophrenic shattering of the atom that destroys everything in its path but also how to slow down and control its nuclear reaction in order to achieve socially desirable ends. The task for psychology is a roughly similar one: to learn enough about the structure of belief systems to know how to form them, and how to modify them so that they will best increase the happiness and freedom of the individual and his society.

TWO

An Experimental Analysis of the Organization of Belief Systems

In collaboration with Joseph Reyher and Richard Wiseman

The empirical findings discussed in the preceding chapter are suggestive rather than definitive, and at best they provide us with only a limited test of the validity of our formulations. The data about the various types of beliefs organized along a central-peripheral dimension include verbal reports of perceived importance of belief, anecdotes, or observations of change in delusional beliefs obtained from a very small number of highly selected mental patients.

In this chapter we describe an experimental approach to the determination of importance of belief—an approach we employed with larger numbers of normal subjects. We tried to modify systematically the five types of belief varying in centrality by hypnotic procedures, and we then determined the effects of such changes on the rest of the belief system.

22

From the preceding analysis of the organization of beliefs along a central-peripheral dimension we can derive several simple hypotheses concerning the effects of pressures to change beliefs varying in centrality. Since five types of beliefs have been postulated, it is reasonable to expect that beliefs within each type would exhibit functionally similar effects—would behave alike—if they are subjected to pressures to change. It is, moreover, expected that more central beliefs would be more resistant to change than less central beliefs because the more central beliefs have more connections and therefore more consequences for other beliefs within the total belief system. The greater the consequences, the greater the effort that would be required to reorganize the content and structural relations among the various beliefs within the system. And the greater the effort, the greater one's motivation to resist such pressures to change. If, however, changes are nevertheless induced in central beliefs, they should have relatively more consequences for the rest of the belief system than would be the case for less central beliefs.

Three specific hypotheses are implied in the above:

1. Types of belief located along a central-peripheral dimension are functionally distinct.
2. The more central a belief the more it will resist change.
3. Changes in central beliefs will produce greater changes in the rest of the belief system than changes in less central beliefs.

To test all three hypotheses within the context of a single experiment, deeply hypnotized subjects were presented with 55 beliefs categorized into the five types previously described. Each of the five sets of beliefs was experimentally manipulated, in turn, by suggesting to the hypnotized subject that he believe the opposite. We then measured the amount of subsequent change in each type of belief, and also the amount of change in all the remaining beliefs.

METHOD

SUBJECTS

Volunteer subjects were drawn from a variety of sources in the summer, fall, and winter of 1960 for an experiment involving

23

hypnosis. They were paid $1.00 per hour. Two criteria were employed to determine whether a volunteer would be retained as an experimental or control subject: the experimenter, who was trained in clinical psychology, judged the subject to be free of serious psychopathology; and the subject evidenced a complete posthypnotic amnesia for material he had read aloud during the hypnotic session, and amnesia for various other hypnotic responses that had been elicited from him, such as catalepsy, automatic movements, and dreams. A posthypnotic amnesia was considered to have been established if the subject was unable to describe any of the hypnotic events when asked "What comes to mind about the session?" and "Are you sure there is nothing that you can remember?" The posthypnotic amnesia was included as a requirement for methodological reasons: to preserve the subject's naïvete, and to maintain the effectiveness of the hypnotic conditioning.

Forty subjects, representing 85 per cent of the volunteers, were retained, 29 as experimental subjects, 13 male and 16 female, and 11 simulating or control subjects, 5 male and 6 female. The mean age of the two groups was the same—about twenty-one years —and the subjects were randomly assigned to experimental and control groups.

The experimental subjects were seen only by Experimenter 1 (R. W.). The control subjects, however, were first seen by Experimenter 2 (J. R.) who informed them as follows: (1) that he, Experimenter 2, was hypnotically conditioning all the subjects for the research project; (2) that after each subject had been conditioned he would be transferred to Experimenter 1; (3) that Experimenter 1 would then be able to induce hypnosis rapidly by counting from one to ten; and (4) that the subject had been randomly chosen to serve as a control subject and, therefore, upon hearing Experimenter 1 count from one to ten, he was to behave as best he could as if he were in a hypnotic trance.

MATERIALS AND APPARATUS

The subject was seated in a comfortable armchair in a soundproof room 10 ft. by 12 ft. in size that contained a polygraph. Electrodes for the galvanic skin response apparatus (GSR) were attached to the subject's first and second fingers of the nonpreferred hand. The experimenter sat to the side and somewhat behind the subject to operate the polygraph equipment without being observed. In this position the experimenter was also able to administer a 55-item Belief Inventory. The items were typed on 55 index cards and were presented to the subject one at a time in one of twelve predetermined random orders.

A tray was placed in front of the subject. On it was a box containing the 55 cards, face down, each card being identified with a number from 1 to 55 (but presented in one of twelve random orders). The tray also contained an answer sheet numbered from 1 to 55. The subject was instructed to pick up the first card, turn it over and read it, rate the item on a +5 to a −5 scale of agreement-disagreement, with the zero point excluded, and record his rating in the appropriate space on the answer sheet. The subject was then instructed to set this card aside, pick up the second card, and then repeat the process for all 55 cards.

THE BELIEF INVENTORY

Each item was a separate belief subsumed under one of the five classes described earlier. There were 11 items representing each type of belief; each item had been selected for its ability to elicit either strong agreement or disagreement. With the exception of Type A beliefs which did not require pretesting because of their incontrovertible, factual nature, the items were selected after pretesting on three pilot groups of college students because they had been found to elicit approximately equally extreme (intense) ratings. Table 2 shows the 55 items employed, broken down into the five types of beliefs.

A few additional comments are in order about how we selected these 55 items. First, the three authors constructed an equal number of items for each type, wherein each item was designed to exemplify one and only one of the five belief types. In only a few instances was there disagreement among the authors, and in such instances the item was discarded and another was substituted, or

25

the disagreement was resolved by rewording the belief statement. A second consideration was that the selected items should permit a test of Hypothesis 3 (as well as of Hypotheses 1 and 2). Hypothesis 3 is concerned with the effects of change in one type of belief on the remaining beliefs. Selection of the 55 items was therefore deliberately guided by the consideration that they should be sufficiently interconnected and have implications for one another, so that a change occurring in one or more beliefs of one type could reasonably be expected to lead to changes in the remaining beliefs. To maximize the likelihood of such connectedness we deliberately selected Type A beliefs that were designed to make salient, by indirection, the subject's identity as an American and to contrast it with a Russian identity. Moreover, to maximize the interconnectedness among the 55 beliefs we deliberately selected other beliefs, wherever possible, with political and religious implications (see Types C and D). We refrained from selecting a more heterogeneous set of beliefs for each class for fear that the subject might not see their implications for one another. Thus, for the 11 Type C beliefs we restricted ourselves primarily to political or religious authority figures and we refrained from broadening the list to include authority figures from the worlds of science, philosophy, literature, entertainment, or sports.

Table 2

The Belief Inventory

Type A: Primitive Beliefs, Unanimous Consensus

1. I was born in (real birthplace).
2. I was born in Moscow, Russia.
3. I am .... years old.
4. My mother's name is Olga Petrov.
5. My father's name is Boris Petrov.
6. I am (give religion).
7. I live in Moscow, Russia.
8. I am an atheist.
9. I am a member of the Communist Party.
10. My name is (S's own name).
11. My name is Ivan (Anna) Petrov.

26

Table 2 (*Cont.*)

Type B: Primitive Beliefs, Zero Consensus

12. I can recall having had sexual feelings when I used to snuggle up to my father and press myself up against his strong, firm body.
13. There are times when I wish that I could have an operation that would change me into a woman (man).
14. I believe that my mother loves me.
15. Sometimes I have a strong urge to kill myself.
16. At the beach I often notice other men (women) who have beautiful sensual bodies and have wished that we could become close friends.
17. I can remember having been very curious and sexually excited about the thought of seeing my mother without clothes on.
18. Sometimes I have been so angry with my father that I would like to kill him.
19. I like myself.
20. I am an effective person.
21. I can recall having had sexual feelings when I used to snuggle up to my mother and press myself against her soft, warm body.
22. Sometimes I have been so angry with my mother that I would like to kill her.

Type C: Authority Beliefs

23. The philosophy of Adolph Hitler is basically a sound one, and I am all for it.
24. The philosophy of Nikita Khrushchev is basically a sound one, and I am all for it.
25. The philosophy of Orval Faubus is basically a sound one, and I am all for it.
26. The philosophy of Dwight Eisenhower is basically a sound one, and I am all for it.
27. The philosophy of the Pope (John XXIII) is basically a sound one, and I am all for it.
28. The philosophy of Abraham Lincoln is basically a sound one, and I am all for it.
29. The philosophy of Jesus Christ is basically a sound one, and I am all for it.

Table 2 (*Cont.*)

30. The philosophy of Karl Marx is basically a sound one, and I am all for it.
31. The philosophy of Fidel Castro is basically a sound one, and I am all for it.
32. The philosophy of Al Capone is basically a sound one, and I am all for it.
33. The philosophy of Benedict Arnold is basically a sound one, and I am all for it.

Type D: Derived Beliefs

34. The Russians were justified in putting down the Hungarian revolt in 1956.
35. Birth control is morally wrong.
36. People can be divided into two distinct groups: the weak and the strong.
37. The Gettysburg Address does not really say anything important.
38. Actually the Nazi Party in Germany accomplished many bad things for the German people, and America is better off without a Nazi Party.
39. I think this country would have been better off if the South had won the Civil War.
40. Boris Pasternak did not really deserve to get the Nobel Prize for his novel, *Dr. Zhivago.*
41. The Ten Commandments are of divine origin.
42. The South should be allowed to work out its own social and political problems without interference by outsiders, not even the Federal Government or the U. S. Supreme Court.
43. What this country needs most, more than laws and political programs, is a few courageous, tireless, devoted leaders whom the people are willing to obey without question.
44. To be absolved of sin, one must confess one's sins to a representative of God.

Type E: Inconsequential Beliefs

45. I think summertime is a much more enjoyable time of the year than winter.

Table 2 (*Cont.*)

46. I would never walk through a revolving door if I had a choice.
47. Participating in college athletic activities is a waste of valuable educational time.
48. The side from which I get out of bed in the morning really does influence how I feel.
49. There is no doubt in my mind that Elizabeth Taylor is more beautiful than Dinah Shore.
50. I believe the trend toward higher specialization, such as in medicine, actually decreases the effectiveness of a profession.
51. It makes a big difference to me whether I bathe with soap that sinks or floats.
52. I think television will eventually destroy the movie industry.
53. In terms of driving safety, it is obvious to me that traffic lights should be located on the corner rather than suspended above the street.
54. All this business about brushing one's teeth, even once a day, is nonsense.
55. "Rock 'n' Roll" music is a good example of the degradation of today's youth.

PREEXPERIMENTAL PROCEDURE

After the subject had been put at ease, hypnosis was induced by eye fixation and deepened by eliciting such phenomena as catalepsies, automatic movements, dreams, hallucinations, and anesthesias. To take advantage of EEG findings (Dement and Kleitman, 1957; Dement and Wolpert, 1958) that there is a return to deeper levels of sleep following a dream, we employed a recently developed "deepening" technique (Wiseman and Reyher, 1962) wherein suggestions were made to the subject that the hypnosis would deepen coincidentally with the termination of hypnotically induced dreams.

Subsequent preexperimental training sessions were scheduled for the purpose of deepening and to provide the subject with practice in reading and talking while hypnotized. Finger electrodes for the GSR were attached to the subject's nonpreferred hand in the next to last training session to allay anxiety about the polygraph. A hand catalepsy was induced to minimize movement artifacts.

During the final training session, which was conducted in

the waking state, the experimenter familiarized the subject with the procedure by having him rate all of the 55 items while he was attached to the polygraph. These data will not be reported here.

EXPERIMENTAL PROCEDURE

Following the preexperimental training sessions, each subject was seen on four separate occasions approximately one week apart. Each of these four sessions consisted of four parts: *Pretest,* wherein the subject filled out the complete Belief Inventory in the waking state, to establish a baseline; *Hypnotic Reversal,* wherein one of four types of beliefs, A or B or C or D, was manipulated by hypnotic suggestion, immediately followed by a rating of these items; *Hypnotic Posttest 1,* wherein the subject, still under hypnosis, filled out the complete Belief Inventory; and *Waking Posttest 2,* wherein the subject filled out the complete Belief Inventory while awake.

Pretest. The subject was seated in the armchair, the finger electrodes were attached, and electrolytic paste was allowed to hydrolize with the skin for 15 to 20 minutes. He was then given the following instructions:

> Now I would like you to go through the cards as you did the other day. To refresh your memory, you will pick up the cards one at a time, starting from the back of the pack. After reading the statement, place it in front of the box and then rate it according to the scale at the bottom of the answer sheet. Just answer them according to your own true feelings about them. When you have finished [with each card] be sure to wait for me to tell you before you go on to the next one.

Hypnotic Reversal procedure. The subject was then hypnotized and instructions were given—in each of the four sessions scheduled a week apart—that were designed to reverse, in turn, the subject's evaluations of one of the four types of beliefs, A, B, C, or D. Over the four experimental sessions the order of manipulations was counterbalanced. In every one of the four Hypnotic Reversals a random subset of five of the 11 Type E beliefs (Inconsequential)

30

were intermingled with the 11 Type A or B or C or D belief items. There are two reasons why Type E items were so intermingled. First, this technique provided yet another baseline, in addition to the prehypnotic baseline, for assessing hypnotic change as a function of centrality. If our hypotheses were valid, the subject should not only respond differentially to Types A, B, C, and D beliefs which were manipulated in four different sessions but they should also respond differentially to the two classes of items presented in a given Hypnotic Reversal session, depending on their centrality. Second, by intermingling Type E with the other items it was possible to effect an economy in the research design; we were able to obtain data on differential change in five types of beliefs from four rather than five experimental sessions.

The instructions were:

> Now, as you continue to sleep I want you to listen carefully, for I am going to tell you something about yourself that will probably ring true, even though you may not be able to understand it. At times we may have thoughts and feelings that are amusing or distressing, but which we can't banish from our mind, no matter how hard we might try. Nod your head if this has happened to you. This is quite natural, and it simply means that you have tendencies to think and feel in ways different from what is customary for you, or different from what you might prefer at the moment. In other words, we all have a potential to become a different person from what we are at present.

> Now I am going to help you learn about this inner potential in you in this way: I am going to give you some of the same statements that you answered a short time ago. As you read each statement, thoughts and feelings opposite to what you had experienced before, to that statement, will well up inside of you. These opposite feelings and throughts will become so strong that they will become overwhelming and you will answer the statement in terms of them. [Repeat last 2 sentences.] Now, in a few minutes, I'm going to tell you to open your eyes and you will find, as you have in the past, that you won't awaken in the slightest.

31

The subject was then asked to open his eyes and respond to all the experimentally manipulated items.

Hypnotic Posttest 1. Following the procedure just described, the subject was again asked to close his eyes and he was given the following instructions:

> As you continue to sleep, I again want you to listen very carefully. The opposite thoughts and feelings to these statements that you just experienced have now become an active, important part of yourself, and will continue to be, even when you are not conscious of them. And, like all important thoughts and feelings that you have, they will be seeking ways to express themselves. This will be true whether or not you are hypnotized, and will continue until I say "That's all for today." At that time, all your normal thoughts and feelings will return. [Repeat paragraph.] Also, when I say, "Just relax for a minute," you will enjoy the opportunity to relax and your mind will seem to go blank. Now, I'm going to give you the same statements that you answered when you first came in today.

The subject was then asked to open his eyes and to respond to the complete Belief Inventory.

Waking Posttest 2. Upon completing the preceding task, the subject was again asked to close his eyes and to listen to the following instructions:

> In a few minutes I'm going to awaken you by counting to five, and even though you will not remember anything about this session after I awaken you, you will continue to experience everything that I told you. You are going to sleep very deeply now, and when you awaken you will feel refreshed and relaxed, feeling as if you have just awakened from a long deep sleep.

Upon awakening, the subject responded once again to the 55-item Belief Inventory. Then the electrodes were removed, and the experimenter gave the posthypnotic signal, "That's all for today," to remove all suggestions and to facilitate the reinstatement of the subject's "normal thoughts and feelings." Arrangements were then made for the next experimental session, and the subject was dismissed.

THE MEASURES

The subject responded to the 55-item Belief Inventory a total of 12 times, three times (Pretest, Hypnotic Posttest 1, Waking Posttest 2) during each of four experimental sessions spaced about a week apart. In addition, the subject responded to 11 Type A, B, C, or D beliefs (with five Type E beliefs always interspersed) immediately following the Hypnotic Reversal instructions. With the Pretest of a given session as a baseline, one set of belief change scores was obtained for each of the remaining three testing conditions.

In addition, the subjects' latency of response and GSR were obtained for each item, thus providing us with three complete sets of data on belief change, latency change, and GSR change (micromhos) under all testing conditions in the four experimental sessions. Latency measures were obtained by activating a signal marker on the polygraph at the moment the subject picked up a belief card and at the moment he rated it on his answer sheet. Latency was the difference (in millimeters) between these two scores.

The average reliability of these measures within and between the four experimental sessions differed considerably from one measure to the other. For the experimental group the average reliability was .79, .30, and .21 for the item ratings, latency, and GSR, respectively, and for the control group the average reliabilities were .73, .33, and .28, respectively.

We suspect that the low reliabilities on latencies and GSR are due to uncontrolled and perhaps random affective reactions to each of the belief statements on the various testing occasions, such as humorous reactions to the statements, feelings of surprise due to novelty, and puzzlement over vague impulses to change one's ratings. Such uncontrolled reactions are less likely to influence ratings of agreement or disagreement with the belief statements.

33

RESULTS

EFFECTIVENESS OF EXPERIMENTAL MANIPULATIONS

Three kinds of data suggest the effectiveness of the experimental manipulations we employed:

Symptomatic behavior in experimental and control groups.
The experimenter kept a written record of the subjects' emotional reactions and also tape-recorded the various sessions. These protocols were subsequently evaluated to determine the presence of types of behavior that could reasonably be considered symptomatic of anxiety or conflict. Coding of the protocols was guided by Reyher's nosology (1961, 1967) for describing symptomatic reactions associated with the stimulation of posthypnotic conflict (for example, autonomic disturbances, tics, disturbances of affect, cognitive confusion, dissociative reactions).

All of the 13 classes of symptoms listed in Reyher's nosology, except 3a, 3c, and 8 (1961, 1967), were manifested by the experimental subjects. To illustrate the genuineness and variety of symptoms elicited from these subjects, we cite below verbatim extracts from six protocols:

No. 1 (Male). "I didn't like that—I didn't like to answer some of those. At the time I was answering I tried to forget and get ready for the next. Felt like I wanted to answer—then something —well, I don't know—like well, I don't care. Some of those questions—I don't feel I felt that way. The more disturbing they were to me—like a rush of blood to my head—glad to get the answer down, I'll tell you that, so I could get on to the next one. On the disturbing ones my arm just seemed to tense up until after I answered it. I just didn't like some of those answers."

No. 2 (Male). "Sort of like being drunk, I could feel myself change. Real strong feelings that you don't just give a damn, but I can feel this changing. My impulses were sort of in conflict and it scared me. In service some guy was drunk and fell in my bed and I punched him. Whenever I'm sleeping and anyone comes near me, I get mad. I had this same feeling when you took the cards from me. As if, they're *my* cards, what are you doing taking them from me? I had to suppress the feeling to punch you. I feel like if a cop stopped me I'd tell him to go to hell."

No. 3 (Female). "It seemed as I read some of these questions that two voices were talking to me. I would start to put down one and know darned well that it isn't right. I'll be darned if I'll put it down. It seems that I want to answer them one way, but it would be lying, and I want to be honest."

No. 4 (Female). "It was mostly after you woke me up. While I was hypnotized one time I started to answer 'yes' to my name being Anna, then I thought, 'Oh, that's not right,' but after you woke me, I seemed to identify with her and felt the way I thought she would feel. I really meant it—felt very aggressive. If anyone asked me I would have felt defiantly that was how I felt about them."

No. 5 (Female). "Sometimes I didn't want to put down what I did but I felt I had to; other times I changed it before putting it down. Sometimes I got a first impulse and followed it. Other times I put down a wrong answer but couldn't change it for some reason. If I thought about it before putting it down I was able to. I had a pain in the middle of my forehead."

No. 6 (Male). "The thing that bothered me was I'd start to put down an answer, then have a fear that it wasn't right. Also, between the questions, the flooring here, I was quite taken up by that (typical wood floor). I began counting boards, maybe to kill time between questions."

Symptomatic reactions such as those illustrated above were obtained from 21 of the 29 experimental subjects but from only one of the 11 control subjects. Although the number of symptoms per experimental subject was relatively few and less intense than those obtained by other hypnotic methods for inducing conflict (Reyher, 1967), the differences in symptomatic reactions between experimental and control subjects were sufficiently clear to establish the greater efficacy of the Hypnotic Reversal condition for the former than for the latter groups.

Latency of response. A second kind of evidence suggesting the effectiveness of the instructions for both experimental and control groups, and the greater effectiveness of the manipulations for the experimental group, is presented in Figure 1, which shows the mean latency of response to the belief statements by the experimental and control groups under the four conditions of testing. Note first the increase in response latency from the Pretest to the Hypnotic Reversal conditions of testing for both experimental and control groups, which is significant beyond the .01 level (sign test). While the experimental and control groups did not differ in Pretest response latency, the former exhibited higher latencies than the latter in the three subsequent testings, the differences in the Reversal and in the Posttest 2 testing conditions both being significant beyond the .05 level (Median test). Finally, as one would expect, for both experimental and control groups the response latency decreases steadily (and significantly) from the Reversal to the Hypnotic Posttest 1 to the Waking Posttest 2 conditions of testing.

GSR responses. A third kind of evidence that suggests that the instructions were effective is obtained from the GSR responses of the experimental and control groups, as shown in Figure 2. We note a sharp increase in mean GSR (micromhos) for the experimental group in the Hypnotic Reversal condition of testing, which is significant at the .025 level (sign test). In contrast, the GSR activity of the control group showed marked adaptation in the Reversal condition.

EQUATING OF BELIEF STATEMENTS FOR INITIAL EXTREMENESS

The experimental and control groups were found on the average to rate the various items less extremely on the Pretest than we had originally expected on the basis of results obtained earlier with the pilot groups. The Pretest results obtained for pilot, experimental, and control groups are shown in Table 3. While for the pilot group Types B, C, D, and E items do not differ from one another on extremeness (intensity), there is a systematic inverse relationship between centrality and extremeness for both experimental

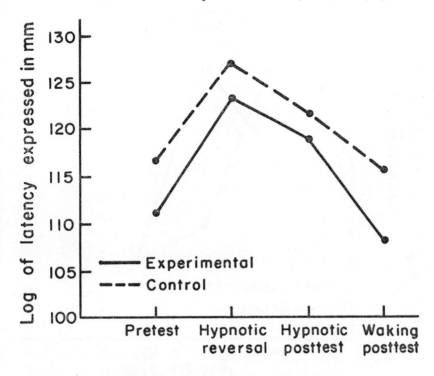

Figure 1. Mean latency of response for experimental and control groups for four testing conditions.

and control groups on the first session's Pretest. We do not know whether the cause of these differences between the pilot group on the one hand and the experimental and control groups on the other was due to the stress of the experimental sessions or to other reasons. We must nevertheless note that while these Pretest findings were not initially equated for intensity, they provide incidental evidence for a positive relation between centrality and extremeness. However, the fact that extremeness is not equated posed a methodological problem that we had to correct since the amount of change possible on a given belief statement is a direct function of the extremeness of its

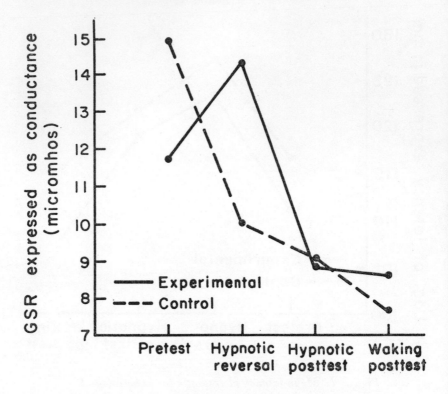

*Figure 2. Mean GSR for experimental and control
groups for four testing conditions.*

initial rating. Furthermore, a comparison of mean change across manipulated types of belief that vary in initial extremeness requires an assumption of equal interval scales, which is untenable.

It was necessary, therefore, to equate the belief types varying in centrality for initial extremeness. This was done by examining each subject's Pretest data and by retaining for analysis, for each subject separately, only those belief statements, within each of the five belief types, which the subject had rated extremely (defined as + or − 4 or 5 on the Pretest). In this way, we were able to equate each of the five belief types for extremeness of ratings, as shown in the last column of Table 3.

Table 3

Mean Pretest Agreement with Five Types of Beliefs by Pilot,
Experimental, and Control Groups before and after Item Selection

| TYPE OF BELIEF | BEFORE ITEM SELECTION | | | | | AFTER ITEM SELECTION | |
| | (A) | (B) | (C) | | | | |
	PILOT GROUP	EXPERIMENTAL	CONTROL	(A-B)	(A-C)	EXPERIMENTAL	CONTROL
A. Primitive, 100%	5.00*	4.60	4.83	.40	.17	4.61	4.85
B. Primitive, 0%	3.61	3.19	3.36	.42	.25	4.38	4.51
C. Authority	3.64	3.09	3.22	.55	.42	4.42	4.76
D. Derived	3.52	2.66	2.66	.86	.86	4.38	4.48
E. Inconsequential	3.34	2.70	2.57	.64	.77	4.36	4.71

* Assumed.

39

With the five types of beliefs thus equated, we then proceeded to test the main hypotheses.

Hypothesis 1: *Types of beliefs located along a central-peripheral dimension are functionally distinct.*

This hypothesis was tested by factor analyzing the obtained change scores—the difference between Pretest and Hypnotic Reversal ratings. This involved a principal axes factor analysis and Verimax rotations to a six-factor solution based upon a 64-variable correlation matrix. Recall that in each of four Hypnotic Reversal testing sessions the subject had rated 16 beliefs—11 each of Type A, or B, or C, or D intermingled with five beliefs randomly selected from the 11 Type E beliefs. This meant that at the end of all four sessions we had change data for 11 beliefs, each of Types A, B, C, and D, plus 20 Type E beliefs randomly selected in subsets of five from the 11 Type E beliefs. If the various types of beliefs located along the central-peripheral dimension are indeed conceptually distinct they should be factorially discriminable. It is important to emphasize, however, that our research design does not permit a distinctive identification of the 20 Type E beliefs because they were manipulated in random subsets of 5 intermingled with Types A, B, C, and D.

The rotated, six-factor solution for the changes thus obtained with the 64 belief statements are shown in Table 4. The six factors account for about 75 per cent of the variance, Factors 1 to 6 accounting for 21, 10, 13, 13, 11, and 6 per cent of the variance, respectively.

Visual inspection of Table 4 shows a rather remarkable congruence between belief types and factors: Type A beliefs typically load on the first factor, Type B on the second, and Type C on the third factor. Type D beliefs typically load on two additional factors —Factors 4 and 5. We are presently unable to identify the difference between these factors.

The 20 Type E beliefs, which cannot be individually identified, do not uniformly load on any one particular factor. We note that five of these items have their highest loading on Factor 6 and that nine others have their highest loadings on Factors 4 or 5. These

40

findings suggest that Factor 6 may be a Type E factor and, furthermore, that those Type E items that do not load on this factor are most likely to load on the two Type D (rather than A, B, or C) factors.

Despite ambiguities of interpretation regarding Factor 6 and regarding the nature of the difference between Factors 4 and 5, it seems reasonable to conclude that the items we have classified on theoretical grounds as belonging to Types A, B, C, and D are, as hypothesized, found to be factorially distinct from one another. It is not possible to include Type E items in the preceding statement, for reasons already stated.

It should be emphasized that the data shown in Table 4 are change data—the difference between ratings on the Pretest and on the Hypnotic Reversal test conditions. If we consider only the 44 beliefs that had been classified on conceptual grounds as Types A, B, C, and D, the data show that 37 of the 44 beliefs have their highest loadings on the predicted factor, while seven do not. Considering each of the belief types separately, we note that every one of the 11 Type A beliefs have their highest loadings on Factor 1; six out of the 11 Type B beliefs have their highest loadings on Factor 2; ten out of the 11 Type C beliefs have their highest loadings on Factor 3; and ten out of the 11 Type D beliefs have their highest loadings on Factors 4 or 5.

The results considered thus far do no more than suggest that the changes in the different kinds of beliefs we have been dealing with (at least, Types A, B, C, and D) are factorially distinct. They do not tell us, however, whether these factorially distinct types of changes in belief arise from systematic differences in the centrality of the various types of beliefs subjected to hypnotically induced changes. We now turn to consider the evidence relevant to Hypothesis 2.

Hypothesis 2: *The more central a belief the more it will resist change.*

Change of belief as a measure of resistance to change. Hypothesis 2 involves a specific prediction that the relative order of

Table 4

Rotated Factor Loadings for Change in 64 Beliefs

ITEM	ROTATED FACTOR LOADINGS					
	1	2	3	4	5	6
A. Primitive, 100%						
1. I was born in	.87	.12	.24	.21	.19	.09
2. I was born in Moscow.	.88	.12	.21	.14	.21	.16
3. I am .... years old.	.84	.11	.26	.22	.19	.07
4. My mother is Olga Petrov.	.93	.05	.25	.05	.06	.04
5. My father is Boris Petrov.	.89	.07	.09	.13	−.01	.06
6. I am .... religion.	.63	.14	.22	.23	.17	.18
7. I live in Moscow.	.90	.07	.18	.12	.15	.14
8. I am an atheist.	.79	.14	.09	.36	−.16	−.03
9. I am a Communist.	.90	.09	.24	−.02	.08	.04
10. My name is	.87	.15	.28	.14	.15	.07
11. My name is Ivan (Anna) Petrov.	.88	.13	.23	.10	.19	.15
B. Primitive, 0%						
12. Sexual feelings toward father.	.34	.40	.38	.57	.43	.03
13. Wish to change sex.	.62	.29	−.13	.03	.04	.03

14.	My mother loves me.	.44	.52	.22	.34	.30	.20
15.	Urge to kill myself.	.23	.80	.25	−.04	.19	−.06
16.	Notice same sex at beach.	.35	.46	.28	.37	.39	−.18
17.	Sexually excited by mother.	.07	.39	.20	.75	−.23	.03
18.	I want to kill my father.	.01	.82	.17	.24	−.01	.05
19.	I like myself.	.22	.46	−.12	.14	.69	.14
20.	I am an effective person.	−.07	.52	−.20	.01	.70	.09
21.	Sexual feelings toward mother.	.06	.64	.27	.51	−.02	−.05
22.	I want to kill my mother.	.42	.60	.33	.16	.23	−.25

C. Authority

23.	Hitler's philosophy is sound.	.42	.28	.72	.17	.16	.05
24.	Khrushchev's philosophy is sound.	.31	.38	.71	.02	.38	.21
25.	Faubus' philosophy is sound.	.43	.20	.49	.37	.45	.19
26.	Eisenhower's philosophy is sound.	.35	.09	.74	.28	−.13	.02
27.	Pope's philosophy is sound.	.22	.34	.56	.32	.25	.15
28.	Lincoln's philosophy is sound.	.16	−.09	.79	.44	.03	.06
29.	Christ's philosophy is sound.	.28	.14	.61	.27	.11	.00
30.	Marx's philosophy is sound.	.17	.53	.26	.06	.19	.58
31.	Castro's philosophy is sound.	.48	.19	.62	.18	.29	.24
32.	Capone's philosophy is sound.	.43	.17	.64	.29	.36	.19
33.	B. Arnold's philosophy is sound.	.20	.03	.81	−.03	.00	.10

Table 4 (*Cont.*)

Rotated Factor Loadings for Change in 64 Beliefs

ITEM	ROTATED FACTOR LOADINGS					
	1	2	3	4	5	6
D. Derived						
34. Russians ok in Hungarian Revol.	.19	-.02	.08	.34	.76	-.04
35. Birth control wrong.	-.11	.16	.11	.46	.39	-.28
36. People are weak or strong.	.19	-.03	.26	.68	.44	.10
37. Gettysburg Address unimportant.	.26	.08	.34	.44	.57	.12
38. Nazi Party bad.	.09	.04	.36	.61	.20	.16
39. South should have won Civil War.	.42	.08	.25	.41	.57	.31
40. Pasternak undeserving of Prize.	.29	.20	.07	.75	.24	.03
41. 10 Commandments of divine origin.	.79	.07	.17	.31	.24	.18
42. U.S. should not interfere in South.	.01	.24	.33	.62	.39	-.03
43. We need tireless leaders.	.35	.01	.23	.25	.40	.27
44. Confession absolves sin.	.21	.17	.35	.57	.52	.27
E. Inconsequential*						
45.	-.06	.20	.33	.10	-.14	.60
46.	.15	.09	.54	-.06	.19	.38

47.	.21	.01	.49	−.02	.63	.13
48.	.07	.08	.34	.05	.42	.68
49.	.44	−.09	.30	.10	.42	.57
50.	.35	.29	−.08	.73	−.05	.10
51.	.48	.09	.28	.40	.10	.03
52.	.28	.41	.18	.18	.53	.04
53.	.22	.66	−.13	.10	−.13	.32
54.	.22	.81	−.03	.07	.24	.27
55.	.21	.06	.24	.62	.40	.18
56.	.32	−.09	.06	.35	.61	.19
57.	.03	−.01	−.26	.65	.20	.21
58.	.10	−.05	.12	.44	.18	.52
59.	.34	.20	.07	.71	.22	.06
60.	.40	−.11	.27	.49	.10	.29
61.	.19	−.38	.46	.50	−.14	.13
62.	.61	.06	.30	.07	.38	.13
63.	.37	.10	.43	.13	.27	.39
64.	.38	.15	−.20	.26	.05	.76

45

*The content of items 45–64 was randomly varied; five of the eleven Type E items were randomly intermingled with Type A beliefs (items 1–11), with Type B beliefs (items 12–22), with Type C beliefs (items 23–33), and Type D beliefs (items 34–44). Identification of specific items is, therefore, not possible.

change among the five types of belief is $A < B < C < D < E$. As already stated, given five types of belief 120 different orders of change are theoretically possible, and the probability of obtaining any one particular order is 1 in 120. Thus, the probability of obtaining the theoretically predicted order is 1 in 120 ($p = .008$), and the probability of obtaining no more than one reversal of one ordinal position from the predicted order is 5 in 120 ($p = .04$). With four classes of belief, 24 different orders are possible and the probability of obtaining the predicted order $A < B < C < D$ is 1 in 24 ($p = .04$). Significant differences in magnitude of change among the five beliefs that are not in the predicted order would not be considered as providing support for Hypothesis 2.

Table 5 shows the findings on amount of change in beliefs as a function of centrality. It is readily apparent that the changes obtained in the experimental group increase systematically from Type A to Type E beliefs. There are no reversals of expected order

Table 5

Mean Changes in Five Types of Belief from Pretest to Hypnotic Reversal and to Hypnotic and Waking Posttests

			TESTING CONDITION		
GROUP	TYPE OF BELIEF EXPERIMENTALLY MANIPULATED	HYPNOTIC REVERSAL	HYPNOTIC POSTTEST 1	WAKING POSTTEST 2	MEAN CHANGE
Experimental	A: Primitive, 100%	2.48	2.66	2.56	2.57
	B: Primitive, 0%	3.50	3.52	2.82	3.28
	C: Authority	3.54	3.47	2.87	3.29
	D: Derived	3.65	3.62	3.55	3.61
	E: Inconsequential	4.25	4.08	3.48	3.94
	Mean Change	3.48	3.47	3.06	
Control	A: Primitive, 100%	4.30	3.94	2.68	3.64
	B: Primitive, 0%	4.09	4.15	3.21	3.81
	C: Authority	4.33	4.49	3.03	3.95
	D: Derived	4.70	4.80	4.44	4.65
	E: Inconsequential	4.27	4.45	3.39	4.03
	Mean Change	4.34	4.37	3.35	

of change in the Hypnotic Reversal condition of testing, there is only one reversal of one ordinal position in the Hypnotic Posttest 1 condition (from Type B to C), and there is one reversal of one ordinal position in the Posthypnotic Posttest 2 condition (from Type D to E). When the results are averaged over all three testing conditions, changes in belief increase systematically from Types A to E without exception. All four sets of results are thus statistically significant—at the .008 level for the Hypnotic Reversal condition, at the .04 level for each of the two Posttest conditions, and at the .008 level for the combined results.

These results differ from those obtained for the control group. The order of changes obtained for the Hypnotic Reversal, the Hypnotic and Waking Posttests are not significant. But the combined means over all three testing conditions do show an order-effect that is significant at the .04 level, thus providing additional support for Hypothesis 2. It should be noted, however, that the control group generally overreacted to all the belief types without regard to centrality, changing significantly more than did the experimental group in the Hypnotic Reversal and in the Hypnotic Posttest 1 conditions of testing (sign test).

Note also that for both experimental and control groups there is a decrease in mean amount of belief change from the Hypnotic Posttest 1 to the Waking Posttest 2 testing conditions. For both groups, these decreases are significant at the .02 level (sign test).

We have tested the validity of Hypothesis 2 in two additional ways: (a) by determining the effects of hypnotic manipulation of a given type of belief upon each of the four remaining types, and (b) by determining the average amount of change in a given type of belief as a result of hypnotically manipulating all the other four belief types. If resistance to change is indeed a direct function of centrality we should expect to find that (a) no matter which type of belief had been experimentally manipulated, the resulting changes in the remaining four types of belief should be inversely related to centrality; (b) the average amount of change produced in a given type of belief as a result of manipulating all other belief types should also be inversely related to centrality.

Table 6 shows that both sets of findings are highly consistent

Table 6

Effect of Manipulation of One Type of Belief on Amount of Change in Remaining Beliefs

CONDITION OF TESTING	TYPE OF BELIEF EXPERIMENTALLY MANIPULATED	MEAN CHANGE IN REMAINING BELIEFS					MEAN	ADJUSTED RATIO
		A	B	C	D	E		
		A. Experimental Group						
Hypnotic Posttest 1	A: Primitive, 100%	(2.66)	2.42	2.70	3.05	3.15	2.83	Mean/A = 1.06
	B: Primitive, 0%	2.73	(3.52)	2.93	2.85	3.59	3.03	Mean/B = .89
	C: Authority	2.65	2.85	(3.47)	3.23	2.95	2.92	Mean/C = .84
	D: Derived	2.74	2.54	3.13	(3.62)	3.08	2.87	Mean/D = .79
	E: Inconsequential					(4.08)		
	Mean	2.71	2.60	2.92	3.04	3.19		
Waking Posttest 2	A: Primitive, 100%	(2.56)	2.21	2.63	2.94	3.04	2.71	Mean/A = 1.06
	B: Primitive, 0%	2.05	(2.82)	2.34	2.45	2.85	2.42	Mean/B = .86
	C: Authority	2.53	2.73	(2.87)	3.30	2.85	2.85	Mean/C = .99
	D: Derived	2.47	2.58	2.80	(3.55)	2.98	2.71	Mean/D = .76
	E: Inconsequential					(3.48)		
	Mean	2.35	2.51	2.59	2.89	2.93		

B. Control Group

		1	2	3	4	5	6	
Hypnotic Posttest 1	A: Primitive, 100%	(3.94)	3.22	4.36	3.74	2.97	3.57	Mean/A = .91
	B: Primitive, 0%	2.34	(4.15)	3.51	3.54	2.63	3.01	Mean/B = .73
	C: Authority	2.31	3.21	(4.49)	3.38	3.51	3.10	Mean/C = .69
	D: Derived	2.34	3.02	3.76	(4.80)	3.23	3.09	Mean/D = .64
	E: Inconsequential					(4.45)		
	Mean	2.33	3.15	3.88	3.55	3.09		
Waking Posttest 2	A: Primitive, 100%	(2.68)	1.97	2.68	2.62	2.61	2.47	Mean/A = .92
	B: Primitive, 0%	1.06	(3.21)	2.05	2.90	1.74	1.94	Mean/B = .60
	C: Authority	.89	2.19	(3.03)	2.18	2.54	1.95	Mean/C = .64
	D: Derived	1.22	1.91	2.41	(4.44)	3.71	2.31	Mean/D = .52
	E: Inconsequential					(3.39)		
	Mean	1.06	2.02	2.38	2.57	2.65		

49

LIBRARY — LUTHERAN SCHOOL OF THEOLOGY AT CHICAGO

with theoretical expectations. Table 6 may be read as follows: When Type A beliefs had been hypnotically manipulated in the experimental group, the mean amount of change obtained in Hypnotic Posttest 1 was 2.66 for Type A beliefs, and was 2.42, 2.70, 3.05, and 3.15 for the remaining Types B, C, D, and E, respectively. In general, the order of change is related to centrality in Posttests 1 and 2. The order-effect is significant ($p = .04$) for Type A beliefs in the Hypnotic Posttest 1 condition and is significant ($p = .04$) for Types A, B, and D beliefs in the Waking Posttest 2 condition of testing.

Let us now look at the column means at the bottom of each of the subsets of data shown in Table 6. These show the mean amount of change obtained for a given type of belief as a result of hypnotic manipulations of all the other belief types. Thus, the experimental group's mean change in Type A beliefs on Posttest 1 was 2.71 as a result of having manipulated belief Types B, C, and D. Similarly, the mean change in Types B, C, D, and E beliefs was 2.60, 2.92, 3.04, and 3.19, respectively, as a result of having manipulated all other belief types. A glance at these means shows a generally steady increase in amount of change from Types A to E, that is, an inverse relationship with centrality. There is one reversal of one ordinal position from the predicted order on the Hypnotic Posttest 1 ($p = .04$), and there are no reversals from the predicted order in the Waking Posttest 2 ($p = .008$).

The results just presented are for the experimental group. For the control group, the changes also seem to be inversely related to centrality, although these results are by no means as clear as those obtained for the experimental groups. When Type C beliefs were hypnotically manipulated, changes on the Hypnotic Posttest 1 are perfectly ordered in relation to centrality ($p = .04$); when Type D beliefs were hypnotically manipulated, changes on the Waking Posttest 2 are also perfectly ordered ($p = .04$). The column means for Posttest 2 show a perfect ascending order ($p = .008$).

Latency of response as a measure of resistance to change. A second way we tested the hypothesis that more central beliefs are more resistant to change was to determine the subjects' latency of response to the belief statements. We assumed that the more resistant a given belief is to change, the greater should be the response latency. The data are shown in Table 7.

Under all conditions of testing for the experimental group, it is apparent that the more central the belief the greater the obtained response latency. The results are in the perfectly predicted order for the Hypnotic Posttest 1 testing condition ($p = .008$). When

Table 7

Mean Changes in Latency for Five Types of Belief from Pretest
to Hypnotic Reversal and to Hypnotic and Waking Posttests

| | | TESTING CONDITION | | | |
| | | HYPNOTIC REVERSAL | HYPNOTIC POSTTEST 1 | WAKING POSTTEST 2 | |
GROUP	TYPE OF BELIEF				MEAN
Experimental	A: Primitive, 100%	15.23	7.92	2.01	8.39
	B: Primitive, 0%	13.24	5.20	− .33	6.03
	C: Authority	10.07	5.02	−6.93	2.72
	D: Derived	11.40	3.40	−4.72	3.03
	E: Inconsequential	10.09	1.88	−5.64	2.11
	Mean	12.01	4.68	−3.12	
Control	A: Primitive, 100%	11.33	8.47	1.37	7.06
	B: Primitive, 0%	6.04	2.57	.75	3.12
	C: Authority	12.62	7.27	−1.06	6.28
	D: Derived	11.14	3.16	−8.28	2.01
	E: Inconsequential	9.28	1.90	1.43	4.20
	Mean	10.08	4.67	1.16	

the results are averaged across all three testing conditions there is one reversal of one ordinal position from the predicted order ($p = .04$). The comparable data for the control group are not significant.

For both the experimental and control groups there is a significant decrease in latency from the Hypnotic Reversal to the Hypnotic Posttest 1 ($p = .01$, sign test) which, in turn, is significantly different from the Waking Posttest 2 condition of testing ($p = .01$), results which are probably due to adaptation. These results are, of course, consistent with those shown in Figure 1.

51

GSR as a measure of resistance to change. The GSR scores (not shown) were found to be unrelated to centrality of belief. They did not line up as predicted either for the experimental or for the control groups. Some reasons why these data do not support Hypothesis 2 will be considered later.

Changes in beliefs over time. How enduring were the changes in the five types of beliefs subjected to experimental manipulation? Recall that the subjects took part in four experimental sessions about a week apart. In each session, the suggestion was made to the subjects that they change their "thoughts and feelings" with respect to a selected subset of beliefs, and on each occasion the subjects were instructed before they were dismissed to revert to their original system of beliefs. If the subjects had fully reverted to their original belief system we should expect to find that the differences between the Pretests on Sessions I and IV would be minor, random, and nonsignificant. If, on the other hand, the "revert to your original belief system" suggestion was not altogether followed, we should expect, on the basis of our theoretical formulations, to observe enduring changes over time that are systematically related to centrality of belief.

For the experimental group, the mean amount of absolute change from the Pretest of Session I to the Pretest of Session IV was .20, .71, .73, 1.06, and 1.12 for belief Types A, B, C, D, and E, respectively. These results are again in the perfectly predicted order ($p = .008$). The results for the control group showed a similar but weaker trend: .12, .68, .54, .87, and .84, respectively, which is not significant.

We also determined for each type of belief the average correlations between Pretest scores obtained in Sessions I and IV. For the experimental group, the average correlations obtained for Types A, B, C, D, and E beliefs between Sessions I and IV were .89, .77, .76, .69, and .62, respectively. The ordering of these data is again perfectly in line with the theoretically predicted order ($p = .008$) and is consistent with the mean changes observed from Pretest Session I to Pretest Session IV. For the control group, the comparable average correlations also show the expected trend, although once

52

again the order is not significant: .95, .69, .80, .79, and .73, respectively, for belief Types A to E.

Other results. The change data presented above represent differences from the Pretest baseline. A second, more contemporaneous, baseline is the amount of change measured from the Type E items that were intermingled with the other types of items in the Hypnotic Reversal condition of testing. The meaningfulness of this baseline was severely impaired by the elimination from the statistical analysis of those items that did not retain their extreme ratings in the first Pretest condition. This reduced the number of Type E items in the Reversal Condition from five to four or three, and in some cases, to as few as two or one. Despite these limitations the trend of these results is generally similar to those already presented—that is, the more central the items the less they changed in comparison to the Type E items. But these results are generally less clear-cut and generally not as significant as those already presented. To save space, we omit them from further consideration.

Hypothesis 3: *Changes in central beliefs will produce relatively greater changes in the remainder of the belief system than changes in less central beliefs.*

The results relevant to the testing of this hypothesis are also presented in Table 6. The means shown in the right-hand column of the table represent the over-all effects of changes in manipulated beliefs upon the remaining, unmanipulated beliefs. Consider, for example, the Hypnotic Posttest 1 findings for the experimental group following the manipulation of Type A beliefs: the mean Posttest 1 change in Type A beliefs—the manipulated beliefs—was 2.66, and the mean change in all four of the remaining types of belief was 2.83. If we look at the mean changes in the unmanipulated (remaining) beliefs following the manipulation of Types A, B, C, and D (2.83, 3.03, 2.92, 2.87, respectively) it would appear that the results are not in accord with Hypothesis 3. Neither the Posttest 1 means nor the Posttest 2 means seem to show any systematic relationship to centrality; the amount of change found in the rest of the belief system appears to be about the same regardless of the degree of centrality of the beliefs that had been manipulated.

It could be contended that these data (mean changes in remaining beliefs) are not comparable because the amount of change initially obtained for the experimentally manipulated beliefs varying in centrality are not equated. As has been shown, Type A beliefs change least and Type E beliefs change most as a result of the hypnotic manipulation. In order to compare the differential effects of such experimentally induced changes in beliefs varying in centrality upon the rest of the belief system, it is first necessary to hold such induced changes constant.

We therefore adjusted the data shown in Table 6 by multiplying the mean changes obtained for all the unmanipulated beliefs by the corresponding reciprocal of the mean change obtained for the manipulated beliefs. This is equivalent to setting all the diagonals of Table 6 at 1.00 and adjusting all the remaining entries proportionally. The end result is an adjusted ratio, shown in the last column of Table 6, which represents the average amount of change obtained for all the remaining, unmanipulated beliefs relative to the amount of change obtained when Types A, B, C, and D had been, in turn, manipulated.

The adjusted ratio data may be read as follows: For the experimental group, the manipulation of Type A beliefs resulted in Posttest 1 changes in all the remaining beliefs which were 1.06 times as large as the Posttest 1 changes observed in Type A beliefs. In other words, Posttest 1 changes of a magnitude of 1.00 in experimentally manipulated belief Type A were accompanied by changes of mean magnitude 1.06 on the remaining beliefs; the manipulation of Type B beliefs resulted in changes in all the remaining beliefs that were only .89 times as large as those obtained on Type B beliefs. The comparable figures for Types C and D beliefs are .84 and .79, respectively. These data thus suggest that experimental changes in Type A beliefs produced, relatively speaking, the greatest amount of change in the rest of the belief system, followed, in turn, by changes in Types B, C, and D. Since the obtained order of these adjusted ratios is perfectly in line with the theoretically predicted order, an order that could arise by chance only once in 24, the result is statistically significant ($p = .04$).

When we turn to the comparable data obtained for the Waking Posttest 2 the order of effect on the remaining beliefs as a result of manipulation of Types A, B, C, and D are 1.06, .86, .99, and .76, respectively. This order of results is not significant. For the control group, the order of effect on the four types of unmanipulated beliefs are .91, .73, .69, and .64, respectively, for Posttest 1, a result that is significant ($p = .04$). For Posttest 2, the adjusted ratios are .92, .60, .64, and .52, respectively, a result that is not significant.

DISCUSSION

From a methodological standpoint, the present findings suggest, as do also those reported by Rosenberg (1960) and by Stachowiak and Moss (1963), that hypnosis is a highly effective methodological tool for studying the organization and modification of belief and attitudes. From a substantive standpoint, the results reported here provide strong support for the theoretical formulations and the hypotheses derived from them. More specifically, they show that the experimental changes obtained for the five kinds of beliefs are factorially distinct, that short-term and more enduring changes in beliefs are systematically related to centrality, and that changes induced in central beliefs have relatively greater repercussions in the rest of the belief system than changes induced in less central beliefs.

The response latency data generally support the belief change data. Despite the relatively low reliability of the latency data, these, too, strongly support the hypothesis that resistance to change of belief is a function of centrality. But the results obtained with the GSR data were generally negative and were in contrast to the positive results obtained for the belief and latency change data. In view of the positive results obtained for belief and latency change, we are inclined to interpret the negative GSR findings as being due to a combination of reasons: low reliability and adaptation, the novelty, surprise, and perhaps humor seen in the various belief statements, especially the Type E statements. In view of the presence of these uncontrolled variables it was perhaps too much to expect that the GSR response would show systematic relations to centrality in an experimental session wherein 55 items were presented in quick succession on the Pretest, followed by 16 items on the Hypnotic Reversal, followed by 55 items in Posttest 1, and by 55 items on Posttest 2.

A question may be raised about sex differences. Recall that the findings obtained for the experimental group were based on 29 subjects, composed of 13 men and 16 women. As might be expected, the women generally changed more as a result of hypnotic suggestion than did the men, but because of the small number of cases involved the differences did not generally reach acceptable levels of significance. Nevertheless, the results bearing on the hypotheses appeared to be consistent for the men and women considered separately, and they were similar in most respects to those reported here for the combined sample. We have not presented them here in order to save space.

The factor loadings shown in Table 4 provide us with independent evidence about the accuracy of our *a priori* classification of beliefs into classes. Recall that 37 of the 44 beliefs of Types A, B, C, and D were found to have their highest loadings on the predicted factors—a result which would suggest that we were about 85 per cent accurate in classifying these 44 beliefs into the four types.[1] This result is, of course, very significantly beyond chance expectancy. But our accuracy of classification apparently differs from type to type. Since every one of the 11 beliefs that had the highest loading on Factor 1 was a Type A belief, we were apparently 100 per cent accurate in classifying these beliefs as belonging to the same type. Our accuracy in classifying Type B beliefs was, however, much smaller— only 55 per cent; five of the 11 Type B beliefs had their highest loadings on a factor other than the predicted one. For Types C and D beliefs, our accuracy was much better—about 91 per cent; in each case ten of the 11 beliefs had their highest loading on the predicted factor.

[1] Recall also that because of the experimental design we were unable to obtain factor analytic data for the Type E beliefs; we are, consequently, unable to report empirical data on our accuracy in classifying these beliefs.

As we look closely at the seven "deviant" beliefs out of the 44 we are unable to discern a pattern that might suggest to us *post hoc* how we might go about improving our classificatory scheme. In view of the fact that the factor analysis was based on only 29 cases, however, it seems reasonable to suggest that a first step in the interpretation of these results is to see if they can be cross-validated.

Although we have not been altogether accurate in classifying the individual beliefs within each type, the over-all results obtained from the factor analysis as well as the other results reported here establish reasonably well the empirical existence of the five types of beliefs as well as their relative ordering in terms of importance. Our results suggest that certain kinds of beliefs that can be specified in advance are generally more important to a person and that others are less important. Beliefs about such issues as birth control and sin, Communism and fascism, Russia and the South, and beliefs about such personages as Hitler and Khrushchev, Lincoln and Christ do not seem to be among the most deeply held of man's beliefs. More resistant to change, our data suggest, are those taken-for-granted beliefs about self-identity and self-esteem that are incontrovertible either because they are shared by virtually everyone or because they are not at all dependent on social consensus.

The present conceptualization of the five types of belief and generalizations from the results concerning them must, however, be regarded as tentative, and subject to further elaboration and refinement. We have not necessarily sampled randomly or representatively—in Brunswik's sense (1947)—from the total universe of beliefs within the belief system because it is difficult to select such samples from a universe as abstract and as uncatalogued as a person's total belief system. Moreover, there is no good reason to believe that only five kinds of beliefs varying in centrality will be sufficient to handle adequately all the beliefs represented within the belief system. Eagly (1967), for example, has found that beliefs about negative characteristics in oneself are more amenable to change than are beliefs about positive characteristics, and she explains this finding as a function of incentive value. This finding, as well as common-sense considerations, would suggest that Type B beliefs can be further conceived as being composed of two subtypes—B+ and B− types of beliefs—those which are self-enhancing (for example, I believe I am a reasonable person) and those which are self-deflating (for example, I believe I am not attractive). Centrality of belief, then, may be defined not only in terms of cognitive connectedness but also in terms of the extent to which a given belief serves to enhance or deflate the ego.

Let us now consider the possibility of alternative interpretations. There are two facets to this problem: Is it possible to derive the ordering of the five types of beliefs on the basis of variables other than connectedness? Is it possible to offer alternative interpretations of the obtained results?

We have ordered the five types of belief by defining centrality in terms of connectedness and by proposing four criteria for deciding which of two types of beliefs is the more connected. The empirical findings reported here provide independent support for this ordering. The question can be raised, however, whether the same order could not have been derived from such other criteria as intensity of belief, or degree of social consensus, or verifiability of belief, or beliefs representing matters of fact versus matters of taste, or beliefs referring to the self versus others.

All these alternatives can be ruled out for various reasons. As already discussed, the differential results were obtained with the initial intensity of the five classes of beliefs held constant. Inspection of the ordering of the five classes reveals, moreover, that it does not represent a continuum of degree of social consensus, or of verifiability of belief. Nor would "matters of taste" versus "fact," or "self" versus "other" enable us to order all five types of beliefs.

Consider next the possibility of alternative interpretations of the obtained data. The fact that these data had been obtained under hypnosis raises the question of demand characteristics (Orne, 1962). In considering this possibility it must first be noted that this research is not particularly concerned with the nature of hypnosis, but with the theory and measurement of changes in beliefs varying in importance. Hypnosis is here employed as nothing more than a convenient method to study phenomena altogether different from hypnosis. The only possible relevance of the demand characteristic argument is that the subjects might have become aware of the hypotheses under investigation and, perhaps to please the experimenter, they had responded in a manner consistent with these hypotheses.

Several considerations lead us to rule out the demand characteristic hypothesis as a plausible alternative explanation of our various findings. First, consider the differences in results obtained for the experimental and control groups. The subjects in the experimental group generally responded selectively to the belief statements varying in centrality. In contrast, the subjects in the control group, simulating hypnosis, generally overresponded to all beliefs (significantly, when compared with the experimental group) as a result of the experimenter's suggestion that they change their beliefs. The fact that they overresponded could readily be attributable to demand characteristics. But this would hardly account for the differential changes observed in the experimental group, changes that varied systematically with centrality. Nor would it account for the differential changes also occasionally found in the control group's data. Second, we had no *a priori* hypotheses about whether or not we would find evidence for enduring changes over time, yet for both experimental and control groups, we found that changes from the Pretest of Session I to the Pretest of Session IV (three to four weeks later) were inversely related to centrality. Third, we had no special theoretical interest in whether or not we would find a decreasing change from the Hypnotic Reversal to the Hypnotic Posttest 1 to the Waking Posttest 2 conditions of testing. We nevertheless found significant decreases for both the experimental and control groups.

Let us assume, however, that both the experimental and control subjects did in fact respond differentially to the five kinds of beliefs because of demand characteristics. To account for such a discriminating performance it would be necessary to assume that the subject's belief system is so organized that he is able to distinguish clearly among the five kinds of beliefs and, further, that he is able to respond systematically to these beliefs because he is somehow aware of their central-peripheral order. In such an event the find-

59

ings could still be viewed as supporting the present interpretation, and the demand characteristic interpretation of the findings would lose much of its force as an *alternative* interpretation.

A reasonable case, however, can be made out for the demand characteristic explanation to account for the findings relevant to Hypothesis 3 (Changes in central beliefs will produce greater changes in the rest of the belief system than changes in less central beliefs). Recall (Table 6) that the adjusted ratio scores show systematic changes for both experimental and control groups in the Hypnotic Posttest 1 testing condition. Let us assume that the subjects somehow knew that they were expected to change their ratings of the remaining unmanipulated items but that they had no way of knowing how much they were supposed to change as a result of the experimental manipulations. Let us assume further that they therefore decided to change their ratings on the unmanipulated beliefs by a more or less constant amount, regardless of the centrality of the manipulated beliefs. Each of the unmanipulated items (presented in random order) was rated by the subject while he was under some constant pressure (from the instructions) to change, and the amount of change was a function of the centrality of the (unmanipulated) item he was now rating rather than a function of the centrality of the previously manipulated items. If these assumptions are tenable, then the demand characteristic explanation is tenable.

It is difficult to decide between the demand characteristic explanation just posed and an explanation of the data in terms of Hypothesis 3. Pending further research, we are therefore forced to state that while the empirical evidence provides support for Hypothesis 3, the demand characteristic explanation cannot be unequivocally ruled out as an alternative explanation.

In conclusion, we wish to draw attention to one major implication of the present findings. A cursory survey of the attitude change literature reveals that in the great majority of studies the relatively peripheral and inconsequential beliefs and attitudes (Types D or E) rather than the more central ones (Types A, B, or C) are typically brought under experimental investigation. Such beliefs and attitudes are usually studied in isolation and are selected on grounds of convenience and ease of experimental manipulation rather than on grounds of randomness, representativeness, or importance of belief. To the extent that principles of attitude change are empirically based on biased samplings of beliefs and attitudes within the belief systems they cannot lay claim to being general principles of attitude change, since they may not be generalizable to populations of beliefs and attitudes other than those sampled. Rather, we would have to regard them as limited principles of attitude change. Such principles, moreover, would seem to have more application to such fields as propaganda (which is interested primarily in Type D beliefs) and advertising (which is interested primarily in Type E beliefs) than to such fields as education or psychotherapy. If the principles of attitude organization and change are to become more relevant to the concerns of such fields as the latter, we shall have to become more concerned than we have been in the past with the problem of randomness, representativeness, and significance of the beliefs and attitudes brought under experimental investigation.

THREE

Race and Shared Belief as Factors in Social Choice

Here's a puzzler: at least a dozen students with darker skins than James Meredith attend the University of Mississippi. Yet their enrollment caused no trouble and they live in harmony with white undergraduates. Some have been here a long time. They include a number of science majors from India and Pakistan. One of them, A. K. Bej, a 24-year-old Bombay Hindu who came to Ole Miss to get a degree in pharmaceutical chemistry, told this newspaper, "None of us has ever experienced any racial resentment of the kind this unfortunate Negro is going through. I live in a regular dormitory and so do most of my friends. There's never been any trouble that I know of."

University Registrar Robert B. Ellis said: "At present we

have 41 international students on campus, a good share of them
from non-white countries in Asia. We've had such a program as
long as I've been with the university. The visitors are completely
accepted here."

How come race-sensitive Mississippians accept dark-hued foreign-
ers but riot over the presence of one American Negro? "That's
one for the sociologists to figure out," Ellis said.

A white undergraduate at the corner soda shop shrugged and
said: "It's just not the same thing. There weren't any Asiatics
in the Civil War."

(From a news release by correspondent Robert N. Branson to the
Lansing State Journal, dated October 4, 1962)

Thus far we have considered only one major dimension of
belief systems—the central-peripheral dimension. A second dimension, that has been treated in greater detail elsewhere (Rokeach,
1960), is the belief-disbelief dimension: we also tend to organize our
beliefs along a continuum of similarity-dissimilarity, and similarity-
dissimilarity of belief, our findings suggest, provides us with a major
criterion for accepting and rejecting others. This criterion of similarity seems to be a more powerful determinant than any other for
accepting and rejecting others—more powerful than even racial or
ethnic criteria.

Several recent studies support the hypothesis that differences
in belief on important issues are more powerful determinants of
prejudice or discrimination than differences in race or ethnic membership. In questionnaire-type studies white college students in the
North, border states, and the South (Rokeach, Smith, and Evans,
1960; Byrne and Wong, 1962; Rokeach and Rothman, 1965;
Smith, Williams, and Willis, 1967), and white teen-agers in California (Stein, Hardyck, and Smith, 1965) have generally been found
to prefer Negroes with beliefs, values, and personalities similar to
their own (for example, a Negro who believes in God) to whites
with beliefs, values, and personalities dissimilar to their own (for

63

example, a white atheist). More generally, these subjects rate less favorably those, regardless of race, whose belief systems are incongruent with their own than those, regardless of race, whose belief systems are congruent with their own. Rokeach, Smith, and Evans (1960) have reported comparable results with Jewish children; the children of their study rated gentiles whose belief systems were seen as congruent with their own (for example, a gentile who is for Israel) more favorably than they did Jews whose belief systems were seen as incongruent with their own (a Jew who is against Israel). Confirmatory results have also been reported for Negro, Jewish, and gentile teen-agers in a Northeastern city (Stein, 1966); for white junior high school students in North Carolina (Insko and Robinson, 1967) and in Tennessee (Wrightsman, Baxter, and Jackson, 1967); for Negro subjects in Ohio, Tennessee, and Mississippi (Smith, Williams, and Willis, 1967); in a study of the differential friendship and marriage preferences of Filipino subjects for Filipinos, Chinese, Japanese, and Spaniards (Willis and Bulatao, 1967); and in studies of the differential preferences of English and French Canadians in eastern and western Canada for English Canadians, French Canadians, and Canadian Indians of varied beliefs (Martin, 1964; Anderson and Côté, 1966).

There are, however, some exceptions that should be cited. Triandis (1961) has reported race to be more important than religion. In commenting on this research Rokeach (1961) pointed out that the religious descriptions Triandis presented to his subjects were vague or ambiguous. In a later study Triandis and Davis (1965) shift their position somewhat by concluding that belief is a more important determinant than race for less intimate interracial relations while race is the more important determinant for more intimate interracial relations. The study by Willis and Bulatao (1967) suggests that Triandis and Davis are right in a relative sense but wrong in an absolute sense; Willis and Bulatao write: "On the average, belief accounts for about 30 times as much variance as does ethnicity in the friendship ratings, while the corresponding ratio for marriage ratings is about 20" (p. 5). Finally, Smith, Williams, and Willis (1967) report that race and belief are about equally important as determinants of friendship ratings for white subjects in Louisiana.

Generalization from all the findings cited is, however, severely limited by the fact that in all these studies the social stimuli were "paper-and-pencil" stimuli and the discriminatory responses elicited were "paper-and-pencil" responses. To overcome this limitation, we conducted three experiments in which subjects were given the opportunity to discriminate on the basis of race or belief, or both, in real-life situations. These experiments were all alike in basic design. A naïve subject engaged four strangers, confederates of the experimenter, in a group discussion about an important or situationally relevant topic. Two of the confederates were white and two were Negro. One white and one Negro agreed with the subject, and one white and one Negro disagreed with him. The subject was then asked to state a preference for two of the four confederates.

In two of the experiments, conducted on a university campus, the subject chose two of the confederates to join him for a coffee break. In the third experiment, which was conducted in the natural field setting of an employment office, the subjects were actually applying for jobs; each chose two of four "job applicants" he would most like to work with. This third experiment provided the strongest test of our major hypothesis. For one thing, these subjects were unemployed workers (or, occasionally, employed workers seeking to change jobs), not college students. More important, they were under the impression that the procedures to which they were subjected were an integral part of a normal interview procedure, and they were totally unaware that they were participating in an experiment —a condition that can rarely be assured with college students participating in psychological experiments.

Within the basic framework of these experiments we were interested in three additional questions:

Comparison between white and Negro subjects. The field experiment in the employment office included Negro as well as white applicants, and the results obtained from these two groups can be compared. This study was carried out during the winter of 1963–64, a period during which civil rights demonstrations and clashes provided many daily headlines. In this charged atmosphere, would Negroes and whites pick working partners along race lines, or would beliefs relevant to the working situation be a more important determinant of interpersonal choice?

Comparison between subjects high and low in anti-Negro prejudice. Rokeach, Smith, and Evans found that "whether a person is high or low in prejudice against Jews and Negroes [as determined by scores on anti-Semitism and anti-Negro attitude scales], he responds to belief rather than racial or ethnic cues when given an opportunity to do so" (1960, p. 155). In our two campus experiments we also studied the extent to which racial attitudes predict social choice.

Comparison between public and private conditions. If discrimination on the basis of race is institutionalized or if there exists extreme social pressure to discriminate along racial lines (as is most clearly the case in the South or in South Africa), there is virtually no likelihood that social discrimination will occur on the basis of similarity of belief. All the experiments reported here were conducted in the state of Michigan, where patterns of racial discrimination are less institutionalized and less subject to social pressure than they are in the South. Nevertheless, it is reasonable to assume that such pressures are far from absent in Michigan and consequently that our subjects would choose partners differently under public and private conditions. This assumption was tested in the two campus experiments.

PROCEDURES IN THE CAMPUS EXPERIMENTS

Two virtually identical experiments were performed, one in 1961 with 20 white male subjects drawn from an introductory sociology class,[1] the second in 1963–64 with 48 white male subjects drawn from an introductory psychology class. At least ten days before the respective experiments, instructors (not the experimenters) administered a six-item anti-Negro scale (Adorno, *et al.*, 1950, p.

[1] We wish to thank Joe Smucker and Del Dyer, who conducted this experiment and analyzed the data.

142). "High-prejudice" subjects were defined as those who obtained plus scores and "low-prejudice" subjects as those who obtained minus scores on this scale.

The experiment was conducted in two adjacent rooms—one for receiving and interviewing the subjects, the other for group discussion—situated in an isolated wing of a campus building. To avoid suspicion, the confederates arrived separately. After all five participants had arrived, they were seated around a conference table and told that their task was to discuss a controversial topic, to be selected from a list of five topics by their chairman, who was to be chosen by election. The topics were: invasion of Cuba, elimination of fraternities from campus, allowing girls to visit men's dormitories, Bible reading in the schools, and the grading system.

Each participant was first asked to introduce himself; then the subject, by prearrangement, was elected chairman. He selected the topic and then led a 15-minute discussion. One white and one Negro confederate agreed with the subject, and one white and one Negro disagreed. Identification was facilitated by printed name cards, as in TV panel shows. Personality effects on interpersonal choice were randomized by rotating the assignments of each confederate so that if he agreed with one subject he disagreed with the next. On terminating the discussion, the experimenter took the subject into the next room for a private interview. The experimenter displayed a seating chart of the participants and, under the guise of checking his written notes against the subject's judgment, asked the subject to identify the opinions expressed by the participants, thus assuring that the subject remembered their opinions as well as their names.

While the subject looked at the seating chart, the experimenter remarked that the participants would be interviewed individually and that therefore there would be enough time for several of them to take a coffee break; he then asked the subject, as chairman, to select two of the participants to join him for coffee. In half the cases the experimenter specified that they would be served coffee in a private room next door (the *private* condition), in the other half that they would go to the grill in the Student Union Building (the *public* condition), where the coffee would be paid for from research funds. After the subject made his choices he was asked how he had decided on them. The experimenter then explained the purpose of the experiment and pledged the subject to secrecy.

PROCEDURE IN THE FIELD EXPERIMENT

The subjects in the field experiment were 26 Negro and 24 white male applicants for the positions of janitor, laundry worker, attendant, and recreational director at two mental hospitals in Michigan. The level of positions applied for was the same for Negro and white applicants. Experimental sessions were scheduled at the employment offices of the two hospitals on days when several job applicants were to appear for job interviews by prior appointment. All such applicants were included in the sample.

After an applicant had filled out the usual application form, the experimenter, posing as a staff member of the personnel office, accompanied him to a "waiting room" in which the four confederates, posing and dressed and previously trained to play their roles as job applicants, were already "waiting to be interviewed." As the experimenter and the subject entered, two confederates were looking intently at a mimeographed sheet entitled "Problems of working with mental patients," on which five topics were listed: what to do if a patient misses dinner, refuses to shave because of a delusion, takes off his clothes, or asks to change his dining-room seat, and what to do with juvenile offenders. In each case two specific courses of action were provided—one based on a rule, the other a more permissive alternative. The experimenter handed mimeographed sheets to the subject and to those confederates who did not already have them, explaining that "they are used in the training program" and suggesting that the applicants look at them while waiting their turns to be interviewed.

The experimenter then left the room, and the four confederates initiated a "spontaneous" discussion of at least three of the five topics. One white and one Negro confederate defended the permissive position, and one white and one Negro confederate defended

68

the rule-oriented position. As in the campus experiments, confederates alternated positions from one applicant to another. The subject was gradually drawn into the discussion, his opinion being directly solicited if necessary. If the subject was not consistent in choosing either the rule or the permissive course of action in the several situations (and this was true of about half the subjects), the confederates tried to follow him, agreeing or disagreeing with him according to their predetermined assignments.

The experimenter returned after about 12 minutes, announcing that the interviewers were not quite ready yet. He then passed out cards and asked each participant to write the names of the two people in the group whom he would most prefer to work with. Since the applicants did not yet "know" one another's names, they introduced themselves. The experimenter then assured the applicants that their choices would be kept confidential and that this part of the interview procedure was "something new and has nothing to do with your employment interview." While the subject wrote down the two preferred names, each of the other four wrote down the names of the two confederates who agreed with the subject most of the time. This was done to check on whether there had been a slip-up in carrying out the assignments. (There were none.) The experimenter then collected the cards, thanked the applicants, and left. He or the personnel assistant returned shortly afterward to escort the subject to his real interview.

THE CHOICES

Under the experimental conditions described, there were six possible combinations of partners among which the subject could choose:

1. S + O +: two persons who agree with him, one of each race.
2. S − O −: two persons who disagree with him, one of each race.
3. S + S −: two persons of the same race (as the subject), one agreeing, the other disagreeing with him.

69

4. O + O −: two persons of the other race, one agreeing, the other disagreeing.

5. S + O −: one person of his own race who agrees and a second person of the other race who disagrees.

6. S − O +: one person of his own race who disagrees and a second person of the other race who agrees.

It is reasonable to assume that the more frequently our subjects chose Pattern 1 or 2 over the remaining patterns, the more probable it was that they were discriminating (that is, choosing preferentially) on the basis of belief criteria alone; the more frequently they chose Pattern 3 or 4 over the remaining patterns, the more probable it was that they were discriminating on the basis of racial criteria alone; and the more frequently they chose Pattern 5 or 6 over the remaining patterns, the more probable that they were not choosing preferentially on the basis of either race or belief criteria alone.

It is immediately obvious from Table 8 that the six patterns did not appear equally often. This is true for each of the three experiments considered separately, and when the data from all experiments are combined we see that Patterns 1 through 6 were chosen by 47, 4, 7, 7, 22, and 31 subjects, respectively.

The most direct way of assessing the relative effects of congruence of belief and congruence of race, as determinants of personal choice, is to compare the number of subjects who chose two persons of the same belief (Pattern 1) with the number who chose two persons of the same race (Pattern 3). Pattern 1 (S + O +) was chosen twice as often as Pattern 3 (S + S −) in the campus 1961 study, four times as often in the campus 1963–64 study, and 15 times as often in the field study. When the data from all three experiments are combined, we find that Pattern 1 was chosen by 47 subjects and Pattern 3 by only seven—a ratio of almost 7 to 1. Under the conditions described, similarity of belief is clearly a more powerful determinant of interpersonal choice than similarity of race.

Additional support for the initial hypothesis is obtained when we compare Pattern 1 with Pattern 2 and Pattern 3 with Pattern 4. Our subjects preferred two partners who agreed with them to two partners who disagreed with them 4 to 1, 13 to 0, and 30 to 3 in

70

Table 8

Frequency of Choice of Various Race and Belief Patterns in Three Experiments. Each pattern consists of two partners. S, same race as subject; O, other race; +, agreed with subject; −, disagreed with subject.

EXPERIMENTAL GROUP	PATTERN						TOTAL
	(1) S+O+	(2) S−O−	(3) S+S−	(4) O+O−	(5) S+O−	(6) S−O+	
Campus 1961	4	1	2	1	3	9	20
High prejudice	2	1	2	0	2	3	10
Low prejudice	2	0	0	1	1	6	10
Private	0	0	1	0	1	8	10
Public	4	1	1	1	2	1	10
Campus 1963–64	13	0	3	3	15	14	48
High prejudice	5	0	1	2	6	7	21
Low prejudice	8	0	2	1	9	7	27
Private	7	0	1	1	8	7	24
Public	6	0	2	2	7	7	24
Field 1963–64	30	3	2	3	4	8	50
Negro	15	3	1	2	3	2	26
White	15	0	1	1	1	6	24
All groups	47	4	7	7	22	31	118

the three experiments, respectively. Of the 118 subjects in the three experiments, 47 chose two partners who agreed with them and only four chose two partners who disagreed with them. In contrast, seven subjects (out of 118) preferred two partners of their own race (S + S −), and seven preferred two partners of the other race (O + O −).

Clearly, similarity of belief is a far more important basis for choosing partners than dissimilarity of belief; only four subjects out of 118 (instead of the 19 that would be expected by pure chance) chose two partners who disagreed with them (Pattern 2). More surprisingly, only 14 subjects (instead of a theoretically expected 39) chose partners of one race (Patterns 3 and 4), and of these 14, as many chose two partners from the other race as from their own.

Let us consider next the findings with respect to Patterns 5 and 6. A sizable proportion of our subjects—53 of the 118—chose coffee- and work-partners varying in both belief and race; 22 chose Pattern 5 (S + O −) and 31 chose Pattern 6 (S − O +). With respect to these two patterns, we note an important difference between the two campus studies on the one hand and the field study on the other. In each of the campus studies, 60 per cent apparently preferred partners differing from one another in both race and belief, but this was so of only 24 per cent of the subjects in the field study; 60 per cent in the field study chose two partners with beliefs congruent with their own, one white and one Negro. It is not possible to say whether these differences are due to sampling differences between college students and workers; or to the fact that choice of coffee-partners is a "one-shot deal" while choice of work-partners has longer-range implications; or to the fact that the particular issues discussed were related to work in the one case but not in the other. Another interpretation that would seem to fit the data equally well is that while a majority of the work-applicants preferred partners with congruent beliefs (S + O +), a majority of the campus subjects preferred the mixed racial Patterns 1, 5, and 6 (S + O +, S + O −, S − O +), their choices among these patterns being about evenly distributed. This preference for SO patterns must be qualified by the fact that the campus subjects avoided Pattern 2 (S − O −).

72

No matter how one chooses to state the differences between the subjects in the campus and field studies, it is clear that in all three experiments similarity of belief is a considerably more frequent basis of choice than dissimilarity of belief; similarity of race is rarely a basis of choice—considerably less often even than chance, and no more frequently than dissimilarity of race; and similarity of belief is a considerably more frequent basis of choice than similarity of race.

In the campus 1963–64 and field studies, we obtained additional data on the order in which the two confederates were chosen. These data (Table 9) generally confirm the findings already presented. Considering first the campus 1963–64 results, note that although a large proportion of the subjects chose a partner who disagreed as well as one who agreed, two-thirds of those who did so chose first the partner who agreed. In contrast, the first choices of all the subjects were exactly evenly divided between the two races. The comparable findings in the field study are even more decisively in favor of belief rather than race congruence as a determinant of choice. Here a much smaller proportion chose a disagreeing as well as an agreeing partner, and three-quarters of those who did so chose the agreeing partner first. Again, these results are in sharp contrast to those concerning race. All but a few subjects chose partners of both races, and only 40 per cent of them chose the partner of their own race first. These findings are quite consistent for the Negro and white subjects considered separately.

Another interesting finding shown in Table 9 is that in both studies the proportion of choices on the basis of belief congruence decreases from the first to the second choice (in the campus 1963–64 study $\chi^2 = 4.50$, $p < .05$; in the field study $\chi^2 = 3.61$, $p < .10$). No such decreases are, of course, observed with respect to race in the campus study, since the racial choices, being exactly equal on the first choice, are already balanced. In the field study we again note a tendency to balance out the unequal racial choices as the subjects proceed from the first to the second partner. These results enable us to understand better the choice patterns shown in Table 8. It would seem as if many of the subjects, especially the campus sub-

73

Table 9

Order of Choice of Partners in Two Experiments

CHOICE		NUMBER OF SUBJECTS	
FIRST	SECOND	CAMPUS STUDY*	FIELD STUDY
+	+	13	30
+	−	23	13
−	+	12	4
−	−	0	3
S	S	3	2
S	O	21	18
O	S	21	27
O	O	3	3

* 1963–64.

jects, were aware of the basis on which they made their first preferential choice, and being motivated by considerations of fair-mindedness, they were more likely to choose a second partner possessing both belief and racial characteristics opposite to those of the first partner. At the same time the results show that more of the subjects were fair-minded about race than about belief.

COMPARISON BETWEEN WHITE AND NEGRO SUBJECTS

Under the experimental conditions described, that is, when a person possesses situationally relevant information about another person's beliefs, there is little evidence indeed that he will discriminate on the basis of race per se. The question may now be raised whether Negro subjects respond any differently from white subjects when choosing others. James Baldwin, one of the most eloquent spokesmen of the Negro people today, has insisted that white people, even well-meaning liberal white people, cannot understand the perceptions, thoughts, feelings, and desires of the Negro who lives in a white society which oppresses him from birth; as a result of lifelong oppression, the Negro's psychological processes are inevitably different from the white's. If Baldwin's contentions are correct we should find our Negro subjects choosing partners in ways that are significantly different from the ways the whites choose. However, the results presented in Table 8 show that in this experimental situation, at least, Negroes chose partners in ways that were indistinguishable from whites. Fifteen Negro applicants (out of 26) and 15 white applicants (out of 24) chose two partners who agreed with them, one white and one Negro. Only three of the Negro subjects and only two of the white subjects chose two partners of one race, and these were not necessarily of their own race.

COMPARISON BETWEEN SUBJECTS HIGH AND LOW IN PREJUDICE

In the two campus studies the subjects had been classified before the experiment as high or low in prejudice on the basis of an anti-Negro scale. The results of both studies are essentially the same for high- and low-prejudice groups (Table 8). It would seem that scores on an anti-Negro scale are not necessarily related to real-life discrimination.

COMPARISON BETWEEN PUBLIC AND PRIVATE CONDITIONS

In neither campus study did privacy appear to have an effect on racial choice. In 1961, only one out of ten subjects in the private condition and two out of ten in the public condition chose two partners of their own race or of the other race; in 1963–64, two out of 24 in the private condition and four out of 24 in the public condition chose two partners of their own race or of the other race. If we look further at the campus 1963–64 data, it is also evident that the frequency of choice of all six patterns is remarkably similar under the public and private conditions. However, certain unanticipated differences in choice patterns appear between the two conditions in the campus 1961 study. Four subjects in the public condition but none in the private condition chose Pattern 1—two partners who agreed with them; eight subjects in the private condition but only one in the public condition chose Pattern 6—one partner of the same race who disagreed and one of the other race who agreed with the subject. The variability of patterns chosen is generally

75

greater for the public than for the private condition, but it makes for a difference only in the belief choices, not the racial choices. While the difference between conditions is statistically significant ($\chi^2 = 7.27$), we are nevertheless inclined to discount this difference for methodological reasons[2] and to conclude tentatively that the social pressures in a northern campus community were not sufficiently great to produce consistent differences between public and private choices. In support of this interpretation, the naïve subjects were undoubtedly aware that they were participating in interactions with the four others within a university context or an employment-interview context in the State of Michigan, a state that took an early lead in developing nondiscriminatory laws and policies in employment and in education. This may have been sufficient to indicate to them that there existed no strong external social pressures to discriminate along racial lines. In other words, the conditions under which the studies were conducted must have suggested to the subjects that they were more or less free to choose partners in any way thy wanted to.

It is conceivable, of course, that, given the social context, the subjects may have felt some external pressure *not* to discriminate along racial lines. We had no way of determining which or how many subjects may have felt such pressure. In any event, our data show little or no discrimination along racial lines; and, whether or not external pressures not to discriminate along racial lines existed,

---

[2] It is tempting to suggest that these differences are somehow due to the existence of social pressures in the campus community in 1961 and to their disappearance in 1963–64, perhaps as a result of changing social norms concerning civil rights. If this interpretation were valid we would expect to find the campus 1963–64 results under both private and public conditions looking very much like the campus 1961 results found under private conditions, but this does not appear to be the case. A more likely possibility is that the difference between public and private conditions in the campus 1961 study are, because of the small number of cases, unreliable, despite the fact that they turn out to be statistically significant. We are inclined to discount these results because we determined the significance level by first looking at the data then combining Patterns 1 to 5 (in order to eliminate small frequencies) and, more important, because we have not been able to replicate them.

76

the subjects were free to choose from among the remaining five patterns.

Our main interest in studying differences in discrimination patterns under public and private conditions stems from the assumption that the crucial social-psychological difference between them is the presence or absence of social pressures to coerce discrimination along racial lines. It is interesting to speculate about the results we might have obtained had we been able to replicate our studies in the deep South. An attempt to set up such a study in the deep South was unsuccessful, mainly because of anticipated reprisals toward research collaborators, confederates, and cooperating subjects. Had such a study proved feasible we would have predicted results considerably different from those reported here, namely, that because of greater social pressures existing under public than under private conditions, choice of coffee- and work-partners would have been more uniformly along racial rather than belief lines.

Regarding the role of belief versus race as a determinant of discrimination, Triandis (1961) and Stein, Hardyck, and Smith (1965) have raised the objection that in the vast majority of social situations where discrimination is practiced (for example, in employment, education, public transportation and accommodation, and housing) white people do not inquire into the beliefs of Negroes to determine whether they are congruent or incongruent with their own. The person discriminated against is a total stranger whose belief system is unknown to the person doing the discriminating. We have already suggested that discrimination along racial lines can be expected to occur whenever there is sufficient social pressure or when it is institutionally sanctioned. Under such conditions beliefs are irrelevant as a basis for discrimination. What should be added is that white persons in general and prejudiced white persons in particular, as a result of living within a social system in which racial discrimination is socially reinforced, come to assume that Negro strangers possess beliefs, values, and personalities dissimilar to their own. Thus, Byrne and Wong (1962) found in a group of white subjects in Texas that those with anti-Negro prejudice more frequently than those without assumed that Negroes' beliefs are dis-

77

similar to their own. Similarly, Stein, Hardyck, and Smith have reported (1965, p. 288) that "the correlations presented . . . seem to indicate that the inference made by most subjects about a Negro teenager, in the absence of other information, is that he is *unlike* them."

A final point concerns the issue of equal-status social contacts. Brink and Harris's (1964) public-opinion data show that whites who have had previous social contact with Negroes are less prejudiced and have fewer stereotypes than whites with no such contact. Many others have pointed out that racial prejudice can be overcome or eliminated if individuals get to know one another in equal-status contacts. Our studies lead to the same conclusion but with one important qualification. In the field study especially, all contacts were equal-status contacts, but not all individuals who interacted with one another had congruent beliefs. It should therefore be pointed out that the concept of "equal-status contacts" is not necessarily equivalent to the concept of "contact between individuals with congruent belief systems." Research by Stein (1966) shows that the latter variable is more crucial than the former as a determinant of interpersonal choice.

SUBJECTS' REPORTS ON REASONS FOR CHOICE

At the end of the campus 1963–64 study the subjects were invited to give their reasons for choosing as they did. Four types of reasons were given (Table 10). Since there were no differences between high- and low-prejudice subjects or between subjects in the public and private conditions, these breakdowns are not shown. The most frequent reason given—by 20 out of 48 subjects—was to "keep the discussion going" or some variant thereof ("interesting guys to talk with," "keep things going," "best talkers"). The majority of these 20 subjects had chosen Patterns 5 and 6, combinations in which both race and belief are varied. Four additional subjects who had chosen Patterns 5 and 6 said more or less explicitly that they chose one of each race and one of each belief. When asked why, they responded with such reasons as "because of my Army experience" or "I did not want to leave two Negroes" or "I picked one on color and one on belief."

78

Table 10

Reasons for Choice in Campus 1963–64 Study, by Pattern of Choice

REASON	PATTERN					
	(1) S+O+	(2) S−O−	(3) S+S−	(4) O+O−	(5) S+O−	(6) S−O+
Quality of discussion	2	0	3	2	7	6
Race and belief	0	0	0	0	3	1
Personality	4	0	0	1	4	3
Other	7	0	0	0	1	4

79

A third type of reason was "Nice personality" or "I liked them." A fourth type, which we have classified as "Other," may be interpreted as "evasive." The subject said he "didn't know" or "it didn't matter" or "I picked any two guys" or "I just picked two guys sitting next to me." It is interesting to note that 11 of the 13 subjects who chose Pattern 1 (S + O +) but only 12 of the 29 who chose Patterns 5 and 6 gave the third and fourth kinds of reason. This suggests that different processes underlie different choice patterns and, perhaps more important, that those who chose on the basis of belief congruence were generally more evasive about or unaware of the real reasons for their choices, possibly because choosing others on the basis of belief congruence violates religious and social ideals of tolerance toward those with opposing viewpoints.

CONCLUSION

Our three experiments and some of the others referred to in this chapter suggest that the importance of racial attitudes per se as determinants of racial discrimination have been greatly overestimated and the importance of similarity of beliefs correspondingly underestimated. Whatever racial attitudes our subjects may have had seem to have exerted little or no influence on actual choices in social situations where external pressures to discriminate along racial lines were slight or absent (and pressures *not* to discriminate along racial lines possibly present). Reinforcing these findings is Malof and Lott's finding (1962) that highly prejudiced white subjects significantly reduced their conformity behavior in an Asch-type experiment when they received support from a lone ally, regardless of whether the lone ally was a white or a Negro.

Rokeach has speculated elsewhere (1961) on the basis of earlier findings with paper-and-pencil tests, now reinforced by the experiments here described, that "in those actions not subject to social sanction discrimination along racial or ethnic lines would not take place, not even in the South . . . the *locus* of racial and ethnic discrimination is to be sought in society, not in the individual's psyche. If society's constraints were altogether removed . . . man would still discriminate, if discriminate he must, not in terms of race or ethnic grouping, but in accord with his basic psychological predisposition, characteristic of all human beings, to organize the world of human beings in terms of the principle of belief congruence" (p. 188). In other words, belief congruence will override racial or ethnic congruence except when the perceived cost is too great.

It remains to be seen whether the results of these experiments can be replicated with other kinds of subjects, in other kinds of situations, and in other kinds of cultural and subcultural contexts. Another task for future research is to explore in more detail the personal and social determinants of all the choice patterns we observed.

81

FOUR

The Principle of Belief Congruence and the Congruity Principle

The main purpose of this chapter is to elaborate further the principle of belief congruence discussed in the preceding chapter so that it will apply to instances of cognitive interaction. A second purpose is to compare and contrast the predictions generated by this principle with those generated by Osgood and Tannenbaum's (1955) congruity principle. It will be suggested that the two principles cannot be equally valid since in many instances they appear to lead to contradictory predictions. A third purpose is to present the results of empirical work designed to determine which set of predictions is the more accurate, and a fourth purpose is to try to reconcile the data and interpretations presented by Osgood and his co-workers with those in our own research program.

THE PRINCIPLE OF BELIEF CONGRUENCE

The principle of belief congruence asserts that we tend to value a given belief, subsystem, or system of beliefs in proportion to its degree of congruence with our own belief system and, further, that we tend to value people in proportion to the degree to which they exhibit beliefs, subsystems, or systems of belief congruent with our own. Congruence can be defined both in terms of similarity and importance. Given two beliefs or subsystems of belief equal in importance, the one more similar to our own is the more congruent; conversely, given two beliefs or subsystems perceived to be equally similar to our own, the one judged as more important is the more congruent with our own belief system.

Before discussing how the principle of belief congruence applies to the area of cognitive interaction, it is first necessary to assume that any stimulus (a verbal concept, percept, or event) has the property of activating within a person only a portion of his belief system—that portion that is relevant to or associated with the stimulus. Which particular portion and how broad a portion of the belief system is activated depends on the particular stimulus presented. A particular stimulus may activate only a single belief or a whole subsystem of beliefs varying in breadth or in the number of interrelated component beliefs. KHRUSHCHEV or COMMUNISM, for instance, may activate a broader area of the person's belief system than IVAN PETROV or COLLECTIVE FARM.

Moreover, a person should have no difficulty, when presented with an isolated stimulus, in assessing the direction and importance of the beliefs it activates along any given scale (say, a semantic differential scale) because his previously learned belief system should provide him with a generalized frame of reference for judging direction and importance. The person is able to assess the valence or direction of a particular stimulus by locating the beliefs (or disbeliefs) it activates along the belief-disbelief dimension of similarity-dissimilarity, and he can assess its importance by locating the activated beliefs (or disbeliefs) along the central-peripheral dimension.

Consider now what may reasonably be expected to happen

when one stimulus is associated with another through some assertion. The linkage is assumed to give rise to a unique configuration activating comparison processes designed to determine whether or not there is to be cognitive interaction and, if so, its outcome. An assertion, following Osgood, may be associative or dissociative and may take one of four forms: simple linguistic qualification (LAZY ATHLETE), simple perceptual contiguity (an advertisement showing a MOVIE STAR smoking CAMELS), statements of classification (JONES is a PHYSICIST), and source-object assertions (DE GAULLE opposes TEST BAN). Cognitive interaction refers to the process by which a single evaluative meaning emerges as a result of combining two stimuli, each having their separate meanings.

All the four types of assertions mentioned above have something in common: they are unique configurations cognitively representing a *characterized subject* (*CS*)—a person, thing, or idea characterized or qualified in some unique way. The unique configuration consists of two components: a *subject* (*S*), capable of being characterized in many ways, and a *characterization* (*C*), capable of being applied to many subjects.

Let us now restate the principle of belief congruence in order to apply it to all conditions that might or might not lead to cognitive interaction, and at the same time to predict its outcome quantitatively. Whenever two stimuli are brought into association with one another through an assertion they form a unique configuration activating two comparison processes: the stimuli will first be compared for mutual relevance, and if they are perceived to be at least partially relevant for one another, they will then be compared for relative importance.

COMPARISON OF RELEVANCE

Upon presentation of *CS* a person will first ascertain whether or not the two components, *C* and *S*, are relevant for one another. If he judges them to be not relevant, there are no psychological grounds for expecting cognitive interaction. The irrelevant component should be ignored; that is, it should exert no influence on the evaluation of *CS*. Consequently, *CS* should be evaluated in about the same way the remaining component is evaluated.

COMPARISON OF RELATIVE IMPORTANCE

More interesting for psychological theory and research are those instances wherein a person judges *C* and *S* to be at least partially relevant for one another.

RELATIVE IMPORTANCE OF *C* AND *S*

Under the condition of at least partial relevance, a person will next compare the two components for relative importance with respect to one another, judged within the general frame of reference provided by one's previously learned belief system. And, we conjecture, the evaluation of the configuration *CS* should be a simple average of the evaluations of *C* and *S* considered separately, weighted by the perceived importance of *C* and *S* relative to one another within the context *CS*:

$$d_{cs} = (w)d_c + (1-w)d_s \qquad [1]$$

where d_{cs}, d_c, and d_s refer, respectively, to the degree of polarization (positive or negative) of the characterized subject, the characterization, and the subject, and where (w) and $(1-w)$ refer to the perceived importance of d_c and d_s relative to one another in the context *CS*.

The process described above involves a *paired comparison* of two sets of activated beliefs rather than an absolute judgment and, we conjecture, this paired comparison will be the most crucial determinant of the outcome of cognitive interaction. Further, the evaluative meaning assigned to *CS* will be such that it will be maximally congruent with one's belief system—that is, the precise evaluation of *CS* (positively or negatively) will be a function of its perceived congruence or incongruence with our own belief system; the greater the perceived congruence between *CS* and one's belief system the more positive the evaluation; the less the perceived congruence the more negative the evaluation.

RELATIVE IMPORTANCE OF *CS* AND *C*

When *C* reaches 100 per cent in importance (and *S* 0 per

cent) we must posit the activation of yet an additional comparison process over and above a comparison of C and S, namely, a further comparison of the relative importance of CS and C. Suppose a person perceives IRRESPONSIBLE as all-important in the context IRRESPONSIBLE FATHER. In such a case, it might be reasonable at first glance to assume from Formula 1 that a person's evaluation of CS would be completely determined by his evaluation of C; that is, he evaluates CS the same way he evaluates C. Such an assumption, however, overlooks the possibility that by virtue of the interaction between C and S within the framework of one's total belief system a person's evaluation of CS may be even more extreme than his evaluation of C. He may feel strongly negative toward IRRESPONSIBLE but even more strongly negative toward IRRESPONSIBLE FATHER because he may feel that fathers especially should not be irresponsible. In other words, he may evaluate CS as falling outside the limits of C and S. A characteristic that is negatively evaluated in isolation may be judged even more negatively when it is lodged in a positive subject; conversely, a characteristic that is positively evaluated in isolation may be judged even more positively when it is lodged in a negative subject.[1]

The combined effects of the two comparison processes (C versus S, and CS versus C) on the evaluation of CS under the condition described may be quantitatively expressed as follows:

$$d_{cs} = d_c + (v)d_c \qquad [2]$$

[1] We are dealing here with a comparison process sometimes referred to as *overassimilation*, a process whereby a stimulus not only takes on the valence of another stimulus with which it is associated, but in addition takes on an even stronger valence. This phenomenon can often be observed in everyday life: A Jew who converts to Christianity is sometimes regarded as being "worse" than a *goy*; a positively evaluated person who defects to the other side is even more severely condemned than a negatively evaluated person on the other side (attitude toward the renegade; Rokeach, 1960); a negatively evaluated person who defects to our side is even more warmly embraced than those already on our side.

All the above instances involve a comparison between CS and C. For the sake of completeness the converse possibility should also be mentioned, namely, a comparison process involving the relative importance of CS and S when S is perceived to be 100 per cent important. On intuitive where d_c represents the effect of the first comparison process (C versus S), $(v)d_c$ represents the additional effect of the second comparison process (CS versus C), and v represents the extent to which the person attaches greater importance to CS than he does to C. When the person judges CS to be equal C in importance, $v = 0$ and $d_{cs} = d_c$. When the person judges CS to exceed C in importance, v will equal some coefficient expressing the extent to which CS is perceived to exceed C in importance, and d_{cs} will exceed d_c by the amount (v) d_c. When d_c is positive, d_{cs} will be more positive, and when d_c is negative d_{cs} will be more negative.

One important restriction should be noted here. The value of d_{cs} cannot be allowed to exceed the most extreme score on whatever happens to be the scale of measurement employed in empirical research (for example, ± 3 on a scale ranging from -3 to $+3$), consequently $d_c + (v)d_c$ cannot be allowed to exceed this extreme score either. If d_c, for example, already equals the most extreme score, then the sum of d_c and $(v)d_c$ is arbitrarily assigned the same score.

CONTRAST BETWEEN THE BELIEF CONGRUENCE AND CONGRUITY PRINCIPLES

The formulation of the principle of belief congruence differs from Osgood and Tannenbaum's congruity principle in several important respects.[2]

1. The congruity principle is an additive model that predicts the outcome of cognitive interaction solely from a knowledge of the direction and degree of polarization of the two stimuli considered in isolation. In contrast, the principle of belief congruence is a configurationist model asserting that the comparison processes cannot become activated until the two stimuli are linked together to form a unique gestalt (Asch, 1946, 1952) and, consequently, the outcome

---

grounds, however, this does not appear to be psychologically meaningful and will therefore not be given further consideration here.

[2] The most detailed exposition of the congruity principle will be found in the original article by Osgood and Tannenbaum (1955). For further elaborations, see Osgood, Suci, and Tannenbaum (1957) and Osgood (1960). An excellent summary of this work is given by Brown (1962).

of the cognitive interaction cannot be accurately predicted solely from a knowledge of the direction and intensity of the two stimuli considered separately.

This is not to say, however, that the evaluative meaning of the unique configuration, *CS*, is unpredictable. As already noted, *CS* is evaluated against the general background of one's total belief system. In Chapters One and Two of this volume we attempted to describe various types of beliefs within the belief system and to locate them along a central-peripheral dimension. These formulations provide us with a basis for predicting, at least roughly, the evaluative meaning of any given *CS*: they guide educated guesses about the relative location of beliefs activated by *C* versus *S*, and by *CS* versus *C*, along a central-peripheral dimension.

2. The two principles should yield similar predictions the more discrepant the degree of polarization of the two stimuli considered separately, for the comparison process of relative importance that is activated by the unique configuration will lead to the same discrepant result. On the other hand, the accuracy of predicting the meaning of the configuration from the congruity principle should decrease as the degree of polarization of the separately considered stimuli become more equal to one another. This will be so because the fineness of rating an isolated stimulus along a rating scale (such as the semantic differential) is necessarily limited by the inability of the rater to discriminate reliably more than a small number of points along a continuum (seven points plus or minus two, according to Miller, 1956) which is why most rating scales rarely exceed seven points. On the semantic differential, the method used exclusively by Osgood and his co-workers, only four degrees of polarization are employed (± 3, ± 2, ± 1, and 0). This means that all stimuli, and all beliefs activated by such stimuli, are classified into only four classes, with each class including hundreds or thousands of beliefs necessarily tied in importance (or polarization).

When two equally polarized stimuli are associated together, a finer discrimination regarding their relative importance becomes possible because the comparison process involves the method of paired comparison rather than the method of absolute rating. Thus, the more equally polarized two stimuli are when rated separately the more likely that the comparison process itself will break the tie and, hence, the more inaccurate the congruity principle's prediction of the outcome of cognitive interaction. For example, if one strongly admires COLLEGE PROFESSORS (+3) and equally strongly deplores EXTRAMARITAL SEXUAL RELATIONS (−3) and then learns that the former approves of the latter, the relative importance of the two stimuli can be assessed by a paired comparison, and the perceived size of the discrepancy in importance, determined by the frame of reference provided by one's belief system, will decisively determine the fate of the cognitive interaction. According to the congruity principle, however, the outcome of cognitive interaction between two equally polarized stimuli, one positive and one negative, should be an exact compromise to zero or neutrality, because the congruity principle assumes that the two equally polarized stimuli remain equal whether judged separately or together.

3. The two models differ in their conception about the psychological meaning of incongruity. Exactly what is incongruous with what? According to Osgood and Tannenbaum (1955) the incongruity is between the C and the S, and the greater the disparity between C and S the greater the incongruity and the greater the pressure to reduce it when the assertion is positive; the reverse holds when the assertion is negative. Reduction of incongruity between C and S is achieved by a compromise in which C and S both change toward or away from one another in inverse proportion to their respective degrees of polarization.[3]

The psychological meaning of incongruity is formulated somewhat differently within the belief-congruence framework. The incongruity arises not from the psychological disparity between C

---

[3] The formula Osgood, Suci, and Tannenbaum (1957) use to predict the outcome of cognitive interaction is:

$$d_{cs} = \frac{|d_c|}{|d_c| + |d_s|} \ (d_c) + \frac{|d_s|}{|d_c| + |d_s|} \ (d_s)$$

"where $|d|$ is deviation or polarization from neutrality on the scales regardless of sign, d is deviation from neutrality with respect to sign" (p. 278).

and S but from the disparity between C and CS, or between S and CS, or both. The evaluative meaning of CS must somehow be made maximally congruent with one's belief system, which includes within it previously learned evaluative meanings of C and S. Since CS cannot be completely congruent with both C and S (assuming some discrepancy in the evaluative meaning of C and S), a question arises about the exact process whereby the evaluative meaning of CS will become maximally congruent with C and S. The principle of belief congruence attempts to describe how this outcome comes about. The more discrepant the relative importance of C and S with respect to one another the greater the pressure to evaluate CS, positively or negatively, like C or like S, whichever is the more important, but not both. The more C equals S in importance, the more equalized the pressure from C and S.

4. The congruity principle is essentially a compromise model, the only exception being the following: when an extremely polarized stimulus is positively associated with a neutral stimulus, the meaning of the combined stimuli is assimilated to that of the extremely polarized stimulus. In contrast, the principle of belief congruence allows for various degrees of compromise, and assimilation and over-assimilation depending on the relative importance of C versus S and of C versus CS, in the context CS, regardless of the degree of polarization of C and S, considered separately.

5. The congruity model formally posits an assertion constant in the case of source-object assertions: there is a greater force acting on the object than on the subject; that is, according to Brown (1962, p. 26), "the object of the bond will be *more* affected than the source of the bond." In contrast, the principle of belief congruence denies the necessity of such an assertion constant and states instead that the magnitude of the force acting on the *source* and *object* depends on the relative importance of the beliefs activated by that source and object. For example, in the assertions "KENNEDY praises GOD" and "GOD praises KENNEDY," the congruity principle's assertion constant should lead to the expectation that there will be a greater average change of value on the two objects than on the two sources. In line with the principle of belief congruence we would

90

expect instead that the less important component, whether source or object, would be the more affected.

A TEST OF THE TWO PRINCIPLES

Before presenting the results of empirical work specifically designed to test the contradictory predictions generated by the two principles, attention should first be drawn to a relevant and substantial body of data cited in the preceding chapter. Rokeach, Smith, and Evans (1960), for example, have shown that white subjects in the North and South rate incongruous race-belief configurations such as "Negro who believes in God" and "white person who is an atheist" not by compromise, as the congruity model would predict, but by assimilation, the evaluation of the total configuration CS being more or less completely assimilated to that of C—the belief said to characterize the Negro or white. Similar results were obtained for Jewish children when they were presented with congruous and incongruous configurations depicting Jews and gentiles holding various beliefs. The Jewish children positively evaluated gentiles who agree with their views (for example, a gentile who is for Israel) and negatively evaluated Jews who disagree with their views (for example, a Jew who is against Israel). The total configurations (CS) were evaluated in essentially the same way the belief is evaluated in isolation (C) and, furthermore, regardless of whether the person holding the belief is a Jew or gentile (S). Similarly, Byrne and Wong (1962) and Stein, Hardyck, and Smith (1965) presented fictitious personality profiles of whites and Negroes to their white subjects, some profiles being similar to and some different from the subjects' own profiles. The subjects evaluated positively those having personality profiles similar to their own and evaluated negatively those having profiles different from their own, regardless of whether the profile belonged to a white or Negro.

We may tentatively conclude that the subjects were responding in accord with the principle of belief congruence, which predicts assimilation whenever extremely important characteristics (beliefs or traits) are associated with positively and negatively valued people

Table 11

Mean Error of Predictions and Significance Tests of Differences between Mean Obtained Evaluation Scores for Combined Concept and Means Predicted by the Congruity Model and the Belief-Congruence Model

ASSERTION	M	SD	MEAN ERROR	t
1. A White Person who is a Communist				
Predicted: congruity	3.75	1.41		
Obtained	2.06	1.05	1.69	8.09[a]***
Predicted: belief congruence	2.50	.65	.44	2.44[b]*
2. A White Person who is an Atheist				
Predicted: congruity	4.43	1.43		
Obtained	2.92	1.46	1.51	7.40***
Predicted: belief congruence	3.43	.43	.51	2.22*
3. A Negro who believes in God				
Predicted: congruity	6.32	.97		
Obtained	6.42	.85	.10	.83
Predicted: belief congruence	6.35	.28	.07	.51

4. A Negro who is an Anticommunist	Predicted: congruity	5.96	.98	.07	.50
	Obtained	5.89	1.24	.02	.10
	Predicted: belief congruence	5.91	.12		
5. My Mother is Insincere	Predicted: congruity	4.42	.77	2.38	13.84***
	Obtained	2.04	.96	.42	1.62
	Predicted: belief congruence	2.46	1.60		
6. University Professor favors Extramarital Sexual Relations	Predicted: congruity	4.37	1.40	1.47	5.90***
	Obtained	2.90	1.56	.01	.04
	Predicted: belief congruence	2.89	.75		
7. Clark Gable was in favor of Fidel Castro	Predicted: congruity	3.56	1.21	.94	4.14***
	Obtained	2.62	1.23	.11	.50
	Predicted: belief congruence	2.73	.84		

Table 11 *(Cont.)*

Mean Error of Predictions and Significance Tests of Differences between Mean Obtained Evaluation Scores for Combined Concept and Means Predicted by the Congruity Model and the Belief-Congruence Model

ASSERTION	M	SD	MEAN ERROR	t
8. Dishonest Athlete				
Predicted: congruity	3.36	.88		
Obtained	1.80	.85	1.56	9.28***
Predicted: belief congruence	2.06	.85	.26	1.49
9. Unfaithful Romance				
Predicted: congruity	3.73	.77		
Obtained	2.13	1.19	1.60	8.54***
Predicted: belief congruence	2.52	1.11	.39	1.63
10. Nikita Khrushchev advocates Close Family Ties				
Predicted: congruity	5.25	1.09	.17	.74
Obtained	5.08	1.57		
Predicted: belief congruence	5.54	1.12	.46	1.64

11. Russia extends Freedom of The Press	Predicted: congruity	5.66	1.10	.24	.80
	Obtained	5.42	1.70		
	Predicted: belief congruence	5.55	.88	.13	.45
12. A Prostitute who looks like Grace Kelly	Predicted: congruity	3.90	1.35	1.05	5.97***
	Obtained	2.85	1.58		
	Predicted: belief congruence	4.10	1.53	1.25	3.89***

[a] t tests for correlated measures between obtained and predicted (congruity) scores.
[b] All t's between obtained means and means predicted by the belief-congruence model were corrected for heterogeneity of variance, whenever necessary (Edwards, 1960, pp. 106–108).

 * $p < .05$.
 ** $p < .01$.
 *** $p < .001$.

and not in accord with the congruity principle, which predicts compromise. However, these studies do not provide us with a definitive test of the two principles because they employed research designs somewhat different from those of Osgood and his co-workers, and they did not employ the semantic differential. We therefore designed a new study involving the semantic differential which replicated Osgood and Ferguson's word combination study (Osgood *et al.*, 1957, p. 275) except in one significant respect: we deliberately tried to select various concepts which, when presented separately, would activate more or less highly polarized beliefs, thus ensuring that the predictions regarding the outcome of cognitive interaction by the principle of belief congruence would be diametrically opposed to those made by the congruity principle. As in the Osgood and Ferguson study, we selected components whose combinations were assumed to be credulous, and the purpose of the study was the same as theirs, namely, the prediction of the evaluative meaning of word combinations.[4]

Forty-two white subjects, enrolled in an introductory psychology course at Michigan State University in the summer of 1961, rated 22 component concepts and 12 combinations shown in Tables 11 and 12 on three semantic differential scales representing evaluation (valuable-worthless; admirable-deplorable; good-bad). We used three types of assertions: simple linguistic qualification, statements of classification, and source-object assertions. The subjects first rated the 22 individual concepts on each of the three scales, and then rated 12 assertions linking two concepts. For the exact procedure see Osgood, Suci, and Tannenbaum (1957, p. 275). Predicted evaluation scores ranging from 1 to 7, which is, of course, equivalent to a range from -3 to $+3$, were calculated for each subject separately on the basis of the congruity formula; then, the mean predicted (from the congruity model) and mean obtained scale scores were calculated for all subjects.

[4] Actually, we obtained data on potency and activity as well as on evaluation. Since the evaluative dimension is of major concern to attitude theory and research, only the evaluation data will be reported here.

Table 12

*Mean Differences between the Evaluation of the Combined
Configuration and Each of the Two Components*

	M	MEAN DIFFERENCE	t
1. White Person	5.35		
		3.29	14.95***
A White Person who is a Communist	2.06		
		.39	2.60*
Communist	2.45		
2. White Person	5.35		
		2.42	8.96***
A White Person who is an Atheist	2.92		
		.32	1.78
Atheist	3.24		
3. Negro	5.38		
		1.04	6.50***
A Negro who believes in God	6.42		
		.10	.91
God	6.52		
4. Negro	5.38		
		.51	2.83**
A Negro who is an Anticommunist	5.89		
		.07	.39
Anticommunist	5.96		
5. My Mother	6.51		
		4.47	19.60***
My Mother is Insincere	2.04		
		.18	1.38
Insincere	1.86		
6. University Professor	5.85		
		2.95	8.94***
University Professor favors Extra-marital Sexual Relations	2.90		
		.25	1.32
Extramarital Sexual Relations	2.65		

Table 12 (*Cont.*)

*Mean Differences between the Evaluation of the Combined
Configuration and Each of the Two Components*

	M	MEAN DIFFERENCE	*t*
7. Clark Gable	5.26		
		2.64	9.78***
Clark Gable was in favor of Fidel Castro	2.62		
		.26	1.37
Fidel Castro	2.36		
8. Athlete	5.84		
		4.04	20.20***
Dishonest Athlete	1.80		
		.27	2.25*
Dishonest	1.53		
9. Romance	6.09		
		3.96	17.22***
Unfaithful Romance	2.13		
		.49	2.97**
Unfaithful	1.64		
10. Nikita Khrushchev	3.19		
		1.89	7.56***
Khrushchev advocates Close Family Ties	5.08		
		1.35	5.40***
Close Family Ties	6.43		
11. Russia	4.08		
		1.34	4.19***
Russia extends Freedom Of The Press	5.42		
		.73	2.52*
Freedom Of The Press	6.15		
12. Prostitute	2.33		
		.52	3.25**
Prostitute who looks like Grace Kelly	2.85		
		2.82	10.68***
Grace Kelly	5.67		

* $p < .05$.　　** $p < .01$.　　*** $p < .001$.

Table 11 shows that the obtained means are reasonably close to the congruity model's predicted means in only four out of the 12 combinations (NEGRO who believes in GOD; NEGRO who is an ANTICOMMUNIST; NIKITA KHRUSHCHEV advocates CLOSE FAMILY TIES; RUSSIA extends FREEDOM OF THE PRESS). Statistical tests, shown in Table 11, indicate that the obtained and predicted means for these four assertions are not significantly different from one another, results required by the congruity model. On the other eight assertions, however, the obtained means deviate markedly from the congruity model's predicted means, and in all eight instances are significantly different from one another at the .001 level.

It will be further noted in Table 12 that in the majority of the assertions the evaluative meaning of *CS* deviates markedly from that of *S* and adheres closely to that of *C*. In six out of the 12 assertions (Assertions 2, 3, 4, 5, 6, 7) *CS* does not differ significantly from *C*. In one instance (WHITE PERSON who is a COMMUNIST), *CS* is even more negatively evaluated than *C*, and significantly so—a clear instance of overassimilation. Finally, in Assertions 8 and 9, the evaluative meaning of *CS* is almost but not quite completely assimilated to *C*. When we consider the results of Assertions 1 through 9 all together, the obtained results for *CS* are generally poorly predicted by the congruity principle.[5] Only in the case of Assertions 10 and 11 are the obtained evaluations clearly predicted by the congruity model (Table 11). Finally, only in the case of Assertion 12 is the mean evaluation of *CS* (PROSTITUTE who looks like GRACE KELLY) closer to *S* than to *C*, and here, too, the obtained mean differs significantly from the congruity model's prediction.

[5] In only two of these nine assertions—the two Negro configurations—do the obtained means differ insignificantly from the congruity model's predictions (Table 11). The closeness of predictions in these two instances may be spurious; the disparity between *S* and *C* is very small and, consequently, it is virtually impossible for the obtained results, assuming that they fall somewhere in between the component means, to differ significantly from the results predicted by the congruity principle.

Let us now consider the extent to which the obtained results of *CS* are predicted by the principle of belief congruence which asserts that the relative importance of the two components perceived with respect to one another is the crucial determinant of the evaluative meaning of the combined configuration. To generate specific predictions from this theory it is necessary to have independent measures of relative importance. Since we were not able to obtain such measures on the original sample of 42 subjects (for the simple reason that at the time of this study we had not yet fully developed the model presented here), we obtained the required measures of relative importance on a second comparable sample of introductory psychology students tested in the fall of 1963.[6] We proceeded on the assumptions that the average evaluative meaning of the components considered separately (shown in Table 12) would be approximately the same in the two samples, and that the relative importance of *C* and *S* in the context *CS* would also be approximately the same for the two samples. Thus, we predicted from measures of relative importance obtained from one sample to measures of evaluative meaning of combinations obtained from another, presumably comparable, sample.

The instructions[7] were as follows:

This is a scientific study in the meaning of words and combinations of words. There are no right or wrong answers. What we want is *your* personal opinion.

Consider, for example, the combination "IRRESPONSIBLE FATHER."

1. How do you feel about IRRESPONSIBLE FATHER? On the rating scale below indicate with a check mark how strongly you approve or disapprove of IRRESPONSIBLE FATHER.

[6] We wish to thank Jacob Jacoby for his invaluable help in collecting and analyzing these data.

[7] The quantitative measurement of relative importance proved to be unusually complicated from a technical standpoint. The subjects exhibited considerable difficulty in understanding what was meant by "relative importance." Two preliminary studies were necessary to perfect these instructions.

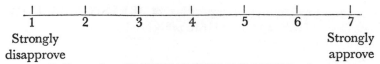

1	2	3	4	5	6	7

Strongly   Strongly
disapprove   approve

2. In rating IRRESPONSIBLE FATHER the way you did, how important, that is, how much weight did each word, IRRESPONSIBLE and FATHER, have in determining your rating of IRRESPONSIBLE FATHER? Did you feel about the combination IRRESPONSIBLE FATHER the same way you felt about the single word IRRESPONSIBLE or the same way you felt about FATHER? Estimate how much weight IRRE-SPONSIBLE and FATHER had in determining the way you actually rated the combination IRRESPONSIBLE FATHER.

(a) My feelings about IRRESPONSIBLE *completely* (100 per cent) determined the way I rated IRRESPONSI-BLE FATHER.

Yes .... Now proceed to question (b).

No .... Now proceed to question (c).

(b) In fact, my feelings about IRRESPONSIBLE FA-THER are even more extreme than my feelings about other people who are IRRESPONSIBLE.

.... No, my feelings about IRRESPONSIBLE FATHER and IRRESPONSIBLE are about of equal strength.

.... Yes, my feelings about IRRESPONSIBLE FATHER are even stronger than my feelings about other people who are IRRESPONSI-BLE.

.... How much stronger? Slightly stronger (1 per cent stronger)? Quite a bit stronger (50 per cent stronger)? Much, much stronger (100 per cent stronger)? My best guess is (fill in blank at left).

Do not answer (c). Go on to the next page.

(c) My feelings about IRRESPONSIBLE did not *completely* determine my rating of the combination IRRE-SPONSIBLE FATHER. I would guess that IRRE-SPONSIBLE influenced me about .... per cent

in determining my rating of IRRESPONSIBLE FA-
THER and FATHER influenced me about ....
per cent.

Two additional examples then followed—GOD-FEARING
THIEF and TRAITOROUS AMERICAN—using the identical
instructions. Then subjects were presented with the 12 assertions
already discussed, in each case using the same "programmed" for-
mat. The order of presentation of the 12 assertions was randomized
from subject to subject.

If the subject responded "No" to Question 2(a) he proceeded to Question 2(c), in which he estimated the relative importance of C and S in percentage terms. However, if the subject
responded "Yes" to Question 2(a) he proceeded to Question 2(b),
thus permitting a determination of whether CS was more important
than C, and if so, how much more important.

The total number of subjects was 71. Of these 14 were
eliminated because they obviously did not understand the instructions: they left one or more questions unanswered, or the two percentage estimates given in Question 2(c) did not add up to 100
per cent, or they answered Question 2(b) when they should have
answered Question 2(c), or vice versa.

Since we did not obtain semantic differential scores for the
components for these subjects we assumed each subject as having
the mean component scores shown in Table 12. We then computed
a predicted score for each combination (CS) for each subject
following Formula 1 or 2, whichever was appropriate. The dis-
tribution of these predicted scores for CS, derived from one group,
were then compared with the obtained CS scores derived from a
comparable group.

It is necessary to emphasize that the results shown in Table
11 are group means. Predictions were actually made for each subject and for each assertion separately. In 38 per cent of all the assertions (a total of 684 assertions) the subjects judged C to be 100 per
cent important and S 0 per cent important) in determining the

102

meaning of *CS* (assimilation); in 16 per cent of all assertions, the subjects further judged *CS* to be more important than *C* (overassimilation) in varying degrees.

The obtained means conform on the whole reasonably closely to those predicted by the belief-congruence model. The obtained means differ significantly from the predicted means in only three of the 12 assertions (1, 2, and 12), and on the remaining nine the obtained means do not differ significantly from the predicted means. In contrast, only four of the 12 obtained means differ insignificantly from the congruity model's predicted means.

A more sensitive test of the predictive power of the two models is obtained by comparing the mean absolute error of the two sets of predictions—the difference between obtained and predicted means. On Assertion 1, for example, the congruity model's mean error is 1.69 while the belief-congruence model's mean absolute error is .44. The mean error prediction for all 12 assertions is 1.07 for the congruity model but only .34 for the belief-congruence model. Thus, the belief-congruence model's average error is only about one-third (.34) that of the congruity model's (1.07).[8]

One possible objection to our procedure is that the predicted and obtained *CS* means were not derived from the same subjects. We therefore also compared the predicted means with the means obtained from Question 1 (see instructions) in which the same subjects evaluated *CS* on a simple seven-point rating scale ranging from "strongly disapprove" to "strongly approve." In other words, obtained means were derived from the subjects' responses to Question 1, and predicted means were derived from their responses to Question 2.

The over-all results are highly similar to those already pre-

---

[8] On the first preliminary study designed to measure relative importance, the mean error for all 12 assertions was .56 ($N = 11$), and on the second preliminary study the mean error was .54 ($N = 63$). The final study, on which the mean error was .34, differs from the preliminary studies in one major respect: it included an evaluative rating of *CS* (see Question 1 on instructions) as well as ratings of relative importance.

sented (Table 11). The mean error of prediction for Assertions 1 through 12 are, respectively: .34, .27, .04, .06, .77, .01, .55, .10, .07, .63, .53, and .82. For all 12 assertions the mean error of prediction is .35.

FURTHER CONSIDERATIONS OF THE VALIDITY OF THE TWO PRINCIPLES

It is clear that the data presented here are considerably more in line with the belief-congruence principle than with the congruity principle. Moreover, the relatively large size of the congruity model's prediction errors appears to be at variance with the results previously presented by Osgood and Tannenbaum (1955) and by Osgood, Suci, and Tannenbaum (1957) in support of their claims for the congruity principle's general validity. In this section we try to reconcile the present findings and interpretations (with respect to the two principles) with those put forward by Osgood and his co-workers, by looking more closely at the evidence they have presented in support of the congruity principle. We suggest that these previously published data provide no more support for the congruity principle than do the present data.

Osgood, Suci, and Tannenbaum (1957) write concerning their word combination study,

> One estimate—perhaps the crudest—is how often the obtained factor scores for the combinations fall between the factor scores for the components, a result required by the congruity formula (p. 280).

In their attitude change study Osgood and Tannenbaum (1955) determine how often "predicted positive changes (+) and predicted negative changes (−) show corresponding signs in the obtained data" (p. 51). The data relevant to such a test, however, do not provide us with any estimate of the congruity model's accuracy other than to tell us that the obtained values have moved some amount greater than zero in the direction of the predicted values—

104

a modest result that could just as easily have been predicted by a much simpler "regression-toward-the-mean" hypothesis.

Osgood, Suci, and Tannenbaum (1957) state,

> Another estimate of the accuracy of prediction is the average magnitude of deviation . . . between predicted and obtained scores for word combinations (p. 280).

They explicitly indicated, after looking at their data, that the congruity formula does not reliably predict the results obtained on the *evaluation* factor.[9] There is therefore no difference between their combination study and ours insofar as the evaluative factor is concerned; neither set of data—theirs or ours—is, considered as a whole, in accord with the congruity model. In this connection we calculated for our evaluation data the correlation between the size of the congruity principle's prediction errors and the magnitude of the disparity between the components and we obtained a rho of +.80. This suggests that the greater the disparity of the two interacting components the less apparent the operation of the congruity principle.

Osgood, Suci, and Tannenbaum (1957) write concerning the Osgood and Ferguson word combination study,

> Still another, and perhaps the best, estimate of prediction accuracy here is the correlation between predicted and obtained mean factor scores . . . . For the evaluative factor, $r = .86$; for the potency factor, $r = .86$; and for the activity factor, $r = .90$.—all highly significant (p. 280).

In their attitude change study, Osgood and Tannenbaum (1955)

---

[9] But, they add, the congruity formula does reliably predict the results obtained on the potency and activity factors. It is highly likely that the disparity of component scores was highly restricted in their study (as it was in the present study), thus making it difficult, if not impossible, for the obtained values to deviate significantly from the predicted values.

report a correlation of .91 between predicted and obtained changes on the evaluation factor.

There are two reasons why we are reluctant to accept these findings as evidence of prediction accuracy. First, it is difficult to reconcile the admittedly negative findings with respect to the evaluation scores discussed above with the high correlations between obtained and predicted scores on the evaluative factor. Second, and far more important, while the high correlations seem at first glance to be impressive evidence for the congruity model, further reflection suggests that the correlations may be spurious. If the upper and lower values of the two components vary from one combination to the next, and if the obtained and predicted values of the combinations fall anywhere between the upper and lower values, a positive correlation will necessarily result even if the two sets of values (predicted and obtained) deviate significantly from one another. For example, the upper and lower limits on Assertion 3 (Table 12) is 6.52 for GOD and 5.38 for NEGRO. Table 11 shows that the predicted and obtained values for the configuration "NEGRO who believes in GOD" fall in between these two values (6.32 and 6.42, respectively). Similarly, the upper and lower limits on Assertion 8 are 5.84 for ATHLETE and 1.53 for DISHONEST, and the predicted and obtained values for DISHONEST ATHLETE again fall in between these values (3.36 and 1.80, respectively). When the two coordinates of Assertions 3 and 8 are plotted on a scatter diagram along with the coordinates for the remaining 10 assertions a high correlation is found ($r = .956$) even though the obtained values differ significantly from the congruity model's predicted values in eight of the 12 assertions. In other words, we, too, get high correlations between obtained and predicted values even though our results for the most part deviate markedly and significantly from those predicted by the congruity principle. Thus the correlation between the obtained and the predicted values cannot provide a test of the accuracy of prediction since the correlation is spuriously influenced by the particular upper and lower values of the two components entering into the combination, which inevitably

106

delimit the range within which the predicted and obtained values of the combination will fall.

CONCLUDING REMARKS

Of all the major balance theories currently extant, the congruity principle is virtually the only one which, until now, has attempted to make specific quantitative predictions regarding the outcome of cognitive interaction. It thus put itself out on a limb where it could more easily be proved inadequate or insufficient. It is to the credit of the authors of the congruity principle that they themselves have drawn attention to the lack of precision in the predictions generated by the congruity model. It is also to their credit that they have tried to improve the predictive efficiency of the congruity model by positing a number of variables that limit its operation, including a quantitative correction for credulity, an assertion constant, and qualitative corrections for relevance-nonrelevance, derogation-nonderogation, and adjective-noun.

In our opinion, all these attempts at improving predictive efficiency stem from the fact that the basic theory on which it is based is psychologically untenable: congruity theory attempts to predict cognitive interaction solely from a knowledge of measurable properties of the components judged in isolation. It is this deficiency that the present formulations are designed to overcome. We think it fair to say that despite the various attempts by Osgood and his co-workers to improve the congruity model's predictive efficiency, their own data do not provide support for the congruity principle, especially with regard to the evaluative factor, the most important factor in semantic differential studies and the one of major interest to attitude theory and research. Consequently, the problem of reconciling our present findings and interpretations, involving the principle of belief congruence, with those of Osgood's would seem to be largely resolved. The data presented here, designed to test the relative predictive efficiency of the congruity principle and the principle of belief congruence, seem to be clearly more consistent with the

107

latter principle. It remains to be seen whether this principle, as formulated earlier (Rokeach, 1960) and further elaborated here, will also prove helpful in studying other phenomena involving cognitive interaction, including attitude change.[10]

[10] The problem of attitude change concerns the effects of cognitive interaction on changing the subsequent evaluative meaning of the components, or those beliefs-disbeliefs activated by the components. While we have presented no data here on this issue it may be assumed, following Osgood and his co-workers, that the principle of belief congruence would predict effects on components, as a function of learning, similar to those predicted for the meaning of word combinations.

FIVE

The Nature of Attitudes

While the preceding chapters are about the nature of belief, this chapter is about the nature of attitude. The concept of attitude is indispensable not only to social psychology, as Allport pointed out in his classic article over thirty years ago (1935), but also to the psychology of personality. My purpose in this chapter is to consider its relevance for personality and social psychology by describing the structure and function of attitudes and the various ways in which attitudes may lead to or determine social behavior. A second purpose of this chapter is to seek a deeper understanding of the nature of attitude by relating it systematically to the concept of belief.

Allport traces three points of origin of the modern concept of attitude: (1) in the experimental psychology of the late nineteenth century which, in its laboratory investigations of reaction-time, perception, memory, judgment, thought and volition, employed such conceptual precursors to attitude as muscular set, task-attitude, *Aufgabe,* mental and motor attitudes, *Einstellung,* and determining tendencies; (2) in psychoanalysis, which emphasized the dynamic and unconscious bases of attitudes; and (3) in sociology, wherein attitudes came to be recognized as the psychological representations of societal and cultural influence. The sociological study of the Polish peasant by Thomas and Znaniecki (1918) is generally credited with being the first to propose that the study of social attitudes is the central task of social psychology, and it was the first to give systematic priority to this concept; but it was not until the 1940's, which began with the publication of Erich Fromm's *Escape from Freedom* (1941) and which ended with *The Authoritarian Personality* (1950), that the relevance of social attitudes for personality theory became widely recognized.

Despite the central position of attitudes in social psychology and personality, the concept has been plagued with ambiguity. As the student pores over and ponders the many definitions of attitude in the literature, he finds it difficult to grasp precisely how they are conceptually similar to or different from one another. Even more important, it is difficult to assess what difference these variations in conceptual definitions make. Most definitions of attitude seem more or less interchangeable insofar as attitude measurement and hypothesis-testing are concerned.

Two critics have gone so far as to suggest that the attitude concept be discarded. Doob (1947) argues that while attitude is a socially useful concept, it has no systematic status as a scientific construct and therefore should be replaced with such learning theory constructs as afferent- and efferent-habit strength, drive, anticipatory and mediating responses. Blumer (1955), writing from a sociological standpoint, recommends abandoning the concept because it is ambiguous, thereby blocking the development of a body of sound social-psychological theory; it is difficult to ascertain what data to include as part of an attitude and what to exclude; it lacks an empirical reference and hence cannot be used effectively as a unit of analysis in either personality organization or the study of social action.

Such views are in the minority, however, and it is safe to predict that the concept of attitude will, despite its ambiguity, remain with us for many years to come. I believe that the confused status of the concept can best be corrected not by abandoning it, but by subjecting it to continued critical analysis with the aim of giving it a more precise conceptual and operational meaning. "At stake," Chein writes, "is not the definition of a word, but the definition of a whole area of psychological inquiry" (1948, p. 187). Katz and Stotland (1959) argue cogently for the attitude concept as follows:

> Efforts to deal with the real world show our need for a concept more flexible and more covert than habit, more specifically oriented to social objects than personality traits, less global than value systems, more directive than beliefs, and more ideational than motive pattern (p. 466).

What exactly is an attitude? What is the conceptual boundary between one attitude and other attitudes? Is it possible to define an attitude in such a way that it is possible to *count* the number of attitudes involved in a particular analysis, or the number of attitudes that may determine a particular social act? At the present state of development of the concept we do not even know how to count attitudes. When we say, for example, that "Such-and-such social behavior is determined by a person's attitudes" we do not know whether we are dealing with two, or ten, or twenty attitudes.

A favorite way to proceed in defining an attitude is to first present a dozen or two definitions from the literature and then, after commenting on their common elements, present one's own with the hope that it is a distillation of the essence of these other definitions. Rather than burden the reader with such an approach, I shall start out with my own definition and, in elaborating upon it, comment on the ways in which it is similar and dissimilar to other conceptions of the nature of attitudes.

111

DEFINITION OF ATTITUDE

An attitude is a relatively enduring organization of beliefs around an object or situation predisposing one to respond in some preferential manner.

AN ATTITUDE IS RELATIVELY ENDURING

Some predispositions are momentary, in which case they are not called attitudes. While such concepts as "set" or *Einstellung* are typically employed in referring to a momentary predisposition, the concept of attitudes is typically reserved for more enduring, persistent organizations of predispositions. It is not possible to differentiate more precisely between temporary and enduring predispositions except to say that a minimum requirement might be test-retest consistency or reliability of measurement. One rarely asks about the reliability of an experimentally induced set, but one always asks about the reliability of an attitude questionnaire. "Attitudes are particularly enduring sets formed by past experiences," Asch writes (1952, p. 585).

While there may be a hereditary basis for attitudes, as Allport (1950) suggests, all writers agree that attitudes are learned through the principles of learning, whatever these are or may prove to be. Along with Sherif and Cantril (1946) and Chein (1948), I believe the definition of an attitude is altogether independent of how it is learned.

AN ATTITUDE IS AN ORGANIZATION OF BELIEFS

Virtually all theorists agree that an attitude is not a basic, irreducible element within the personality, but represents a cluster or syndrome of two or more interrelated elements. Helen B. Lewis emphasizes this view when she defines an attitude as "an interrelated set of opinions organized around a point of reference" (1938, p. 65). In our definition, the elements are underlying beliefs (or cognitions, or expectancies, or hypotheses) rather than expressed opinions.

112

Definition of belief. Jastrow has pointed out that the human "mind is a belief-seeking rather than a fact-seeking apparatus" (1927, p. 284). A belief is any simple proposition, conscious or unconscious, inferred from what a person says or does, capable of being preceded by the phrase "I believe that . . . ." The content of a belief may describe the object of belief as true or false, correct or incorrect; evaluate it as good or bad; or advocate a certain course of action or a certain state of existence as desirable or undesirable. The first kind of belief may be called a *descriptive* or *existential* belief (I believe that the sun rises in the east); the second kind of belief may be called an *evaluative* belief (I believe this ice cream is good); the third kind may be called a *prescriptive* or *exhortatory* belief (I believe it is desirable that children should obey their parents).

Whether or not the content of a belief is to describe, evaluate, or exhort, all beliefs are predispositions to action, and an attitude is thus a set of interrelated predispositions to action organized around an object or situation.

Kerlinger (1967) has pointed out that for two individuals who are said to have an attitude about the same object (for example, Negro, education), different beliefs about the object may be "criterial," or at the center of attention. ". . . what is criterial for one individual may not be criterial for another individual. To be sure, if an attitude is to be an attitude, criterial referents must be shared. But they can be and are differentially shared. That is, we can assume a continuum of relevance for any referent. Group membership, skin color, and civil rights, for instance, can be assumed to be differentially criterial for different individuals" (p. 111).

Each belief within an attitude organization is conceived to have three components: a *cognitive* component, because it represents a person's knowledge, held with varying degrees of certitude, about what is true or false, good or bad, desirable or undesirable; an *affective* component, because under suitable conditions the belief is capable of arousing affect of varying intensity centering around the object of the belief, around other objects (individuals or groups) taking a positive or negative position with respect to the object of

113

belief, or around the belief itself, when its validity is seriously questioned, as in an argument; and a *behavioral* component, because the belief, being a response predisposition of varying threshold, must lead to some action when it is suitably activated. The kind of action it leads to is dictated strictly by the content of the belief. Even a belief that merely describes is a predisposition to action under appropriate conditions. Consider, for example, my belief, "Columbus discovered America in 1492." The behavioral component of this predisposition may remain unactivated until I am one day leafing through two history books to decide which one to buy for my young son. One gives the date as 1492 and the other as 1482. My belief will predispose me, other things equal, to choose the one giving the 1492 date. I am "pro" the 1492-book, and "con" the 1482-book.

Harding, Kutner, Proshansky, and Chein (1954) point out that the relationship among these components is so close that it makes little difference which ones are used to rank individuals with respect to their attitudes toward specific ethnic groups. In experimental research, one component of a belief is difficult, if not impossible, to isolate and to manipulate independently from a second component. Rosenberg (1960), for example, has tried to alter the affective component of a belief under hypnosis in order to determine its effect on the cognitive component. Such an approach assumes that the independent variable can be manipulated without at the same time manipulating the dependent variable. It is equally likely, however, that the effect on the "dependent" variable is not a consequence but a concomitant of the experimental manipulation of the "independent" variable.

Rosenberg's research is only one of many carried out in recent years in which such concepts as balance, harmony, strain toward symmetry, congruity and dissonance play important theoretical roles. All such theories share the common assumption that man strives to maintain consistency among the cognitive, affective, and behavioral components within a single belief, among two or more related beliefs, among all the beliefs entering into an attitude organization, and among all the beliefs and attitudes entering into a total system of beliefs.

114

Distinction between belief and attitude. The conception of an attitude as an organization of beliefs is consistent with Krech and Crutchfield's (1948) view that all attitudes incorporate beliefs, but not all beliefs are necessarily a part of attitudes. The definition departs from one widely-held distinction between belief and attitude, namely that beliefs have only a cognitive component while attitudes have both cognitive and affective components. As Krech and Crutchfield put it: ". . . attitudes can be designated as either 'pro' or 'anti' while beliefs are conceived of as 'neutral.' We speak of a pro-British attitude or an anti-Russian attitude, but we do not speak of pro or con when we are describing a man's belief about the spherical nature of the earth" (1948, p. 153).

There are several grounds for objecting to such a conceptual distinction between belief and attitude. First, Osgood, Suci, and Tannenbaum (1957) and many others have shown that virtually any concept factorially loads on an evaluative dimension, the dimension which, Katz and Stotland state, operationally differentiates the concept of attitude from that of belief, and which, furthermore, "always includes cognitive and affective elements" (1959, p. 428). In this connection, it is interesting to note that the distinction Krech and Crutchfield drew between belief and attitude no longer appears in the revised edition by Krech, Crutchfield, and Ballachey (1962); and in discussing the cognitive component of attitudes, they emphasize mainly the "evaluative beliefs." In a somewhat parallel fashion, Fishbein and Raven (1962) originally distinguished attitude from belief by attributing the evaluative component to attitude and the cognitive component to belief, but this distinction is not maintained in later work: all beliefs are conceived to have evaluative as well as cognitive components (Fishbein, 1963, 1967). Second, any belief considered singly, representing as it does a predisposition to respond in a preferential way to the object of the belief, can be said to have an affective as well as a cognitive component. This affective component will not become manifest under all conditions (for example, every single time a white Southerner sees a Negro) but only when the belief is somehow challenged by the attitude object or by someone else (for example, a Negro asks to be served in a restaurant) or

115

unless the preferential action toward which one is predisposed is somehow blocked (for example, my travel agent violates my belief by routing me from New York to Chicago via London). We do not speak of "pro" or "con" in the case of many beliefs (for example, the shape of the earth) because such beliefs, enjoying universal consensus, do not come up in a controversial way, with everyone preferring the same "pro-round" response. The affective component of such predispositions is typically not activated. Nevertheless the affective component must be assumed to be there, and if and when such a belief becomes a matter of controversy, it will become activated. For example, centuries ago most people believed the earth was flat. When this "pro-flat" belief was challenged by the "anti-flats" the response was undoubtedly far from affectively neutral. Any taken-for-granted belief, however impersonal, has the property of generating affective reactions when its validity is challenged, if for no other reason than that it raises questions about the person's ability to appraise reality correctly. We care about the correctness of our beliefs; truth is good and falsity is bad.

Third, it is not necessary to assume that the positive or negative affect associated with a belief or attitude is necessarily directed toward the object of that belief or attitude. The affect may be directed toward other objects—individuals or groups who agree with us or oppose us with respect to the object—or it may arise from our efforts to preserve the validity of the belief itself.

On the basis of the preceding considerations, an attitude is defined simply as an organization of interrelated beliefs around a common object, with certain aspects of the object being at the focus of attention for some persons, and other aspects for other persons. The attitude has cognitive and affective properties by virtue of the fact that the several beliefs comprising it have cognitive and affective properties that interact and reinforce one another. Newcomb, Turner, and Converse have put it well when they write: "The attitude concept seems to reflect quite faithfully the primary form in which past experience is summed, stored, and organized in the individual as he approaches any new situation" (1965, pp. 41–42).

The concept of organization.   There are a number of structural dimensions frequently employed to describe the organization of several interdependent parts within a whole. These dimensions can with more or less equal ease be employed to describe the organization of (1) the several beliefs contained within an attitude, (2) several attitudes within a more inclusive attitude system, or (3) all of man's beliefs, attitudes, and values within his total cognitive system. It should perhaps be stressed that a change in one part produces cognitive strain or inconsistency within the system, thus giving rise to forces leading to reorganizations in the whole system.

Differentiation refers to the degree of articulation of the various parts within a whole, and the greater the number of parts, the greater the degree of differentiation. A concept used more or less synonymously with differentiation is complexity or multiplexity. Degree of differentiation is an index of the total amount of correct and incorrect information or knowledge possessed about the focus of the attitude. In a paranoid system an attitude may be highly differentiated, but is not necessarily correct. Smith, Bruner, and White (1956) distinguish between degree of differentiation, a phenomenological concept, from its objective counterpart, degree of *informational support*.

Cognitive differentiation also implies a cognitive *integration* of whatever parts are differentiated; there is an appreciation of similarities as well as of differences among parts. We speak of *isolation* or *segregation* or *compartmentalization* of parts within a psychological whole whenever two or more parts within a whole are not functionally integrated or are not seen to be interrelated with one another, or wherein their contradictory nature is not perceived. Levinson (Adorno, *et al.*, 1950), for example, describes the isolated structure of anti-Semitic attitudes: the Jew is believed to be seclusive, but also intrusive; the Jew is believed to be a capitalist, but also a Communist.

Another organizational variable is *centrality*. The parts are conceived to be arranged along a central-peripheral dimension wherein the more central parts are more salient or important, more resistant to change, and, if changed, exert relatively greater effects on other parts.

117

Organization in terms of *time perspective* refers to the extent to which the whole or the part is viewed in terms of the historical past, present, or future and the interrelations among past, present, and future. A time perspective may be broad or narrow. An attitude may have a narrow time perspective in the sense that the beliefs comprising it are oriented primarily in terms of the historical past, or present, or future.

Specificity or *generality* refers to the extent to which one can predict from a knowledge of one belief to another within an attitude organization (for example, from a belief about desegregating the Negro in education to a belief about desegregating the Negro in housing), from one attitude to another (from attitude toward the Jew to attitude toward the Negro), or from the verbal expression of a belief or attitude to nonverbal behavior. It is assumed that specificity-generality of behavior is a function of the degree of differentiation, integration, and isolation of one belief from another, and of one attitude from another.

Breadth or *narrowness* of an attitude or a system of beliefs refers not to the number of parts within a whole but to category width or to the total range or spectrum of relevant social reality actually represented within the whole. An attitude toward Russia, for example, may be broad (for example, covering many facets of Russian life) but relatively poorly differentiated, or it may be narrow (for example, covering only political freedom in Russia) and at the same time highly differentiated.

AN ATTITUDE IS ORGANIZED AROUND AN OBJECT OR A SITUATION

In the first case we refer to an attitude object, a static object of regard, concrete or abstract, such as a person, a group, an institution, or an issue. In the second case we have in mind a specific situation, a *dynamic* event or activity, around which a person organizes a set of interrelated beliefs about how to behave.

Attitude theorists have generally been more interested in the theory and measurement of attitudes toward objects, across situations, than in the theory and measurement of attitudes toward situations, across objects. We have, for example, scales that measure atti-

118

tudes toward the Negro, the church, labor, and socialism. We do not have scales that measure attitudes toward such situations as managing or eating in a restaurant, being a passenger or driver of a bus, buying or selling real estate. As a result, the study of attitudes-toward-situations has become more or less split off from the study of attitudes-toward-objects. To account for the characteristic ways people behave in specific social situations, altogether new concepts are introduced, personality psychologists typically preferring *trait* concepts, and social psychologists preferring *role* concepts and such additional concepts as group norm, social pressure, legal constraints, definition-of-the-situation, and social structure.

The splitting-off of attitude-toward-situation from attitude-toward-object has, in the writer's opinion, severely retarded the growth of attitude theory. For one thing, it has resulted in a failure to appreciate that an attitude object is always encountered within some situation, about which we also have an organized attitude. It has resulted in unsophisticated attempts to predict behavior accurately on the basis of a single attitude-toward-object, ignoring the equally relevant attitude-toward-situation. And it has resulted in unjustified interpretations and conclusions to the effect that there is often an inconsistency between attitudes and behavior, or a lack of dependence of behavior on attitudes.

A more detailed consideration of the relation between attitudes and behavior is reserved for a later section.

AN ATTITUDE IS A SET OF INTERRELATED PREDISPOSITIONS TO RESPOND

Not all writers agree that attitudes are predispositions (or preparations, or states of readiness) to respond. Horowitz (1944) sees an attitude as "a response rather than a set to respond." Doob (1947), analyzing an attitude from the standpoint of behavior theory, sees it as an implicit response. Most writers, however, agree that an attitude is a predisposition of some sort, although there is some difference of opinion about what kind of predisposition it is: predisposition to respond; predisposition to evaluate; predisposition toward an evaluative response; predisposition to experience, to be motivated, and to act. In the present formulation, we prefer simply "predisposition to respond" with the understanding that a response may be either a verbal expression of an opinion or some form of nonverbal behavior. And, following Campbell (1963), attitudes are acquired behavioral dispositions differing from other behavioral dispositions, like habit, motive, trace, and cell assembly, in also representing a person's knowledge or view of the world.

The present formulation differs from other dispositional formulations in one important respect. An attitude, representing as it does an organization of beliefs, is not a single predisposition but a set of interrelated predispositions focused on an attitude object or situation. Not all of these predispositions need necessarily become activated by an attitude object or situation. Which ones are activated depends on the particular situation within which a particular attitude object is encountered. For example, encountering a Negro on a bus in Montgomery, Alabama, will not necessarily activate the same predispositions as encountering a Negro on a bus in Paris, or in a restaurant, or in a dance hall, and consequently will not necessarily lead to the same response toward the attitude object.

Another way in which the present formulation differs from other formulations is that all attitudes are here assumed to be "agendas for action" or to have a behavioral component because all the beliefs comprising them, regardless of whether they describe, evaluate, or advocate, represent predispositions which, when activated, will lead to a response. This formulation differs from Chein's (1948), Smith, Bruner, and White's (1956), and Katz and Stotland's (1959), who all hold that an attitude may or may not have a behavioral component. "For example," the latter write, "one may regard impressionistic art as desirable but not go to a museum of modern art, read about impressionism, or acquire prints of impressionistic paintings. An individual who has an attitude with a behavioral component, on the other hand, has some degree of impulsion to do something to or about the object" (p. 429).

I suggest that such an attitude toward art must also have a behavioral component because the individual holding it must have made some response from which this attitude was inferred. Perhaps he had said something about it in a particular situation; perhaps he had looked admiringly at an impressionistic painting when visiting a friend; perhaps he was impelled to argue about it. If he had said or done absolutely nothing about it, it is difficult to see how anyone could have inferred that he possessed this attitude. A predisposition that does not lead to some response cannot be detected.

AN ATTITUDE LEADS TO A PREFERENTIAL RESPONSE

While everyone agrees that an attitude leads to a preferential (or discriminatory) response, the basis for the preferential response is not clear. Is a positive or negative preference due to the fact that the attitude object or situation is affectively liked or disliked, or because it is cognitively evaluated as good or bad? In most discussions on attitude it is assumed that the two dimensions—affection and evaluation—are more or less synonymous. Katz and Stotland (1959), for example, define attitude as a "predisposition to evaluate," include the cognitive and affective elements under evaluation, and operationally define evaluation in terms of verbal statements of goodness-badness. Osgood, Suci, and Tannenbaum (1957) define attitude as synonymous with the evaluative dimension of the semantic space. Krech, Crutchfield, and Ballachey (1962), while they distinguish the affective component from evaluative beliefs (which are included under the cognitive component), seem to assume implicitly that affection and evaluation generally go together to produce a favorable or unfavorable attitude.

The conceptual difficulty arises from the fact that the two dimensions of *like-dislike* and *goodness-badness* need not necessarily go together. In speaking of the "pro-con" dimension, often said to be *the* defining characteristic of attitude, we do not know whether the preferential response of approach or avoidance is due to the fact that it is liked or disliked or because it is seen to be good or bad. It is possible to like something bad, and to dislike something good. A person may believe, for example, that T. S. Eliot's poetry is good, but he does not like it; or that a particular medicine is good, but he

121

dislikes the way it tastes; conversely, he may believe cigarette-smoking is bad, but he enjoys it. Clearly, there is no necessary one-to-one relation between affect and evaluation. Whether the preferential response will be positive or negative will depend on the relative strength of one's evaluative beliefs and one's positive or negative feelings. A person will make a "pro" response to an object toward which he harbors negative feelings if he believes the object to be sufficiently good for him.

The definition, therefore, emphasizes that an attitude predisposes one to make a preferential response and avoids the implication that the response itself is either affective or evaluative. It may, and usually does, involve both (both positive or both negative), or it may be a resolution of opposing forces between affection and evaluation. Accurate prediction of the preferential response therefore requires a separate assessment of affective and evaluative predispositions underlying the response.

Toward what may the preferential response be directed? An attitude predisposes one to respond preferentially not only to the attitude object or situation, but also to other objects—individuals and groups who agree with or oppose us with respect to the attitude. A favorable or unfavorable attitude toward a presidential candidate, for example, not only predisposes us to respond preferentially to such a candidate on Election Day, but also toward all others who take an attitudinal position with respect to such a candidate. Finally, the preferential response may be directed toward the maintenance or preservation of the attitude itself. A person with a particular attitude is predisposed selectively to perceive, recognize, judge, interpret, learn, forget, recall, and think in ways congruent with his attitude; such selective responses, while mediated by an attitude, are not necessarily responses directed toward the attitude object or situation itself.

A final point is that all three types of responses—toward attitude objects, toward other objects, and toward the maintenance of the attitude itself—may be expected to be positively intercorrelated because they are all mediated by the same attitude.

ATTITUDE DIFFERENTIATED FROM OTHER CONCEPTS

A major source of conceptual confusion arises from the fact that there is considerable disagreement over how the concept of attitude should be distinguished from closely related concepts. Allport points out that "attitude has a wide range of application, from the momentary mental set . . . to the most inclusive . . . dispositions, such as a philosophy of life. This broad usage can neither be denied nor remedied" (1935, p. 806). I venture to suggest that this "broad usage" can and must be remedied. What follows is an attempt to differentiate among various concepts that arise in discussions of attitude, in the hope of giving each of them a more precise meaning.

A *belief system* represents the total universe of a person's beliefs about the physical world, the social world, and the self. It is conceived as being organized along several dimensions (Rokeach, 1960), and additional dimensions can be added as required by further analysis or empirical research. A belief system can further be analyzed in terms of subsystems of varying breadth or narrowness. An attitude is one type of subsystem of beliefs, organized around an object or situation which is, in turn, embedded within a larger subsystem, and so on.[1]

The concept of belief system is broader than ideology, containing pre-ideological as well as ideological beliefs. An *ideology* is an organization of beliefs and attitudes—religious, political or philo-

---

[1] "Attitudes may also be part of a larger psychological structure, in this way interconnected in various degrees with other attitudes, with values, or embedded within an ideology. A person may hold an elaborate system of beliefs the substance of which is that government has no place in the private lives of its citizens as individuals, while recognizing public health as a governmental institution. This ideology may foster negative attitudes toward public health programs concerning smoking, air pollution, immunization clinics, and so forth. Or certain religious beliefs may lead to negative attitudes and opposition to family planning. Most attitudes are connected in some degree to a larger system of thought or beliefs and form and change on this basis" (Knutson, 1965, p. 297).

123

sophical in nature—that is more or less institutionalized or shared with others, deriving from external authority.

The concept of *value* has at least three distinct meanings. To Thomas and Znaniecki, value is a sociological concept, a natural object that has, in fact, acquired social meaning and, consequently, "is or may be an object of activity" (1918, p. 21). To Campbell (1963), Jones and Gerard (1967), and to many others a value seems to be synonymous with attitude because the attitude object has *valence* or cathexis. In this conception, a person has as many values as there are valenced or cathected attitude objects. To many others, including the present writer, a value is seen to be a disposition of a person just like an attitude, but more basic than an attitude, often underlying it.

I consider a value to be a type of belief, centrally located within one's total belief system, about how one ought or ought not to behave, or about some end-state of existence worth or not worth attaining. Values are thus abstract ideals, positive or negative, not tied to any specific attitude object or situation, representing a person's beliefs about ideal modes of conduct and ideal terminal goals —what Lovejoy (1950) calls generalized adjectival and terminal values. Some examples of ideal modes of conduct are to seek truth and beauty, to be clean and orderly, to behave with sincerity, justice, reason, compassion, humility, respect, honor, and loyalty. Some examples of ideal goals or end-states are security, happiness, freedom, equality, ecstasy, fame, power, and states of grace and salvation. A person's values, like all beliefs, may be consciously conceived or unconsciously held, and must be inferred from what a person says or does.

An adult probably has tens or hundreds of thousands of beliefs, thousands of attitudes, but only dozens of values. A *value system* is a hierarchical organization—a rank ordering—of ideals or values in terms of importance. To one person truth, beauty, and freedom may be at the top of the list, and thrift, order, and cleanliness at the bottom; to another person, the order may be reversed. The Allport-Vernon-Lindzey Scale of Values (1960) enables one to measure the relative order of importance of six *classes* of values: theoretical, social, political, religious, aesthetic, and economic.

An *opinion* is here defined as a verbal expression of some belief, attitude, or value.[2] Which underlying belief, attitude, or value the opinion reflects is a matter of inference. The expressed opinion "I am opposed to segregation" may be a manifestation of an underlying attitude about civil rights or an underlying attitude about complying with Federal law, or the teachings of one's church. There are many reasons why a particular verbal expression cannot necessarily be taken at face value. A person may be unable or unwilling to reveal to himself or to others his real (underlying) beliefs, attitudes, or values. He may need to conceal from himself, for example, his idealization of power and transform it, by a process of rationalization, into ideals of charity and responsibility. In the literature, a distinction is often made between *public* and *private* attitudes, and similar distinctions can also be made between public and private beliefs and values. An opinion typically represents a public belief, attitude, or value, but may come closer to private ones when verbally expressed under increasing conditions of privacy.

Faith refers to one or more beliefs a person accepts as true, good, or desirable, regardless of social consensus or objective evidence, which are perceived as irrelevant. A *delusion* is a belief held on faith judged by an external observer to have no objective basis and which is, in fact, wrong. A *stereotype* is a socially shared belief that describes an attitude object in an oversimplified or undifferentiated manner; the attitude object is said to prefer certain modes of conduct which, by implication, are judged to be socially desirable or undesirable (for example, "Negroes are lazy," implying, of course, that Negroes possess a value not shared by the person who is doing

[2] Thurstone and Chave define opinion as "a verbal expression of attitude . . . . An opinion symbolizes an attitude . . . . We shall use opinions as the means for measuring attitudes" (1929, p. 7). The present conception differs from Thurstone and Chave's in viewing an opinion as a possible expression of a belief or value as well as an attitude, and also in viewing an opinion as being a possible manifestation of an attitude of altogether different content.

125

the stereotyping). In contrast to a delusion, a person's stereotype may contain an element of truth in it, but the stereotype is not qualified in any way.

The concept of *sentiment,* which has had a long history, has fallen into general disuse in the past decade or two. Most writers (for example, Murray and Morgan, 1945) agree that sentiment is more or less synonymous with attitude. Asch (1952), however, talks of sentiments as if they are closer to what we have here called values. Insofar as operational definition and measurement are concerned, sentiment and attitude seem indistinguishable.

ATTITUDES AND BEHAVIOR

A preferential response toward an attitude object cannot occur in a vacuum. It must necessarily be elicited within the context of some social situation about which we also have attitudes. It is perhaps helpful to conceive of any particular attitude object as the *figure* and the situation in which it is encountered as the *ground.* How a person will behave with respect to an object-within-a-situation will therefore depend, on the one hand, on the particular beliefs or predispositions activated by the attitude object and, on the other hand, by the beliefs or predispositions activated by the situation. We thus postulate that a person's social behavior must always be mediated by at least two types of attitudes—one activated by the object, the other activated by the situation.

If one focuses only on attitude-toward-object one is bound to observe some inconsistency between attitude and behavior or, at least, a lack of dependence of behavior on attitude. Most frequently mentioned as evidence in this connection are such studies as those by LaPiere (1934) and Kutner, *et al.* (1952), in which there were found to be marked discrepancies among restaurant-owners and innkeepers between their verbal expressions of discrimination toward Chinese and Negro via letter or phone and their nondiscriminatory face-to-face behavior. One possible explanation of such apparent inconsistency is suggested by the present analysis: the investigators did not obtain all the relevant attitudinal information needed to make accurate predictions. The subjects not only had attitudes toward Chinese and Negroes but, being managers of an ongoing business, also had attitudes about how properly to conduct such a business. The investigator's methods, however, are typically focused on obtaining data relevant to attitude-toward-object and are generally insensitive toward attitude-toward-situation.

One may thus readily agree with Krech, Crutchfield, and Ballachey when they say "action is determined, not by a single attitude, but by a number of attitudes, wants, and situational conditions" (1962, p. 163). Their additional statement, however, does not necessarily follow from the preceding: "Attitude test scores alone are usually not enough to predict behavior" (p. 163). As already suggested, a "situational condition" can psychologically be reformulated as "attitude-toward-situation" and assessed by methods similar to those employed in assessing attitude-toward-object. Unfortunately, however, only the latter kind of attitude has thus far been the focus of operational definition and measurement, even though attitudes have typically been more broadly defined as predispositions toward situations as well as toward objects.

Some social psychologists are fond of saying that social behavior is determined not only by "attitudes" but also by the "situation," or by the interaction between "attitude" and "situation." This formulation is conceptually unsatisfactory because "attitude," a psychological variable, and "situation," an objective (sociological) variable, are not from the same universe of discourse. It is meaningless to speak of two concepts that represent different universes of discourse as "interacting" with one another.

A somewhat more satisfactory formulation is the proposition that behavior is a result of the interaction between "attitude" and "definition of the situation" (Thomas and Znaniecki, 1918). The two concepts are, at least, both psychological in nature. This formulation can be improved upon, however, if the two concepts are more directly coordinated with one another. If we assume that "definition of the situation" is at least roughly equivalent to "attitude-toward-situation," then the relation between attitudes and behavior can be formulated as follows: behavior is a function of the interaction be-

127

tween two attitudes—attitude-toward-object and attitude-toward-situation.

The recognition that the two kinds of attitudes will cognitively interact with one another implies that they will have differing degrees of importance with respect to one another, thereby resulting in behavior that will be differentially influenced by the two kinds of attitudes. In one case, an attitude object may activate relatively more powerful beliefs than those activated by the situation, thereby accounting for the generality of behavior with respect to an attitude object; on the other hand, the situation may activate the more powerful beliefs, thereby accounting for the specificity of behavior with respect to an attitude object. Campbell (1963) has shown that the threshold of discrimination toward Chinese seeking reservations for overnight lodging and restaurants is without exception lower—there is more discrimination—in non-face-to-face-situations. He has similarly shown that the threshold of discrimination toward Negro miners by white miners is always lower in town than in the mines (Minard, 1952). In pointing to "different situational thresholds" Campbell (1963) is not only explaining away the apparent inconsistency between attitude and behavior, or between one behavior and another, but he is also suggesting that certain situations, because of the greater social pressures inherent in them, consistently activate discriminatory behavior toward a specific attitude object more than do other situations.

Chein (1948, p. 178) has stated: "People may act contrary to their attitudes." Is this possible? In the present view, I do not see how this is possible. If a person acts contrary to one attitude it must mean that he acted in accord with a second (or third or fourth) attitude that overrode the first attitude in importance. When there is a negative correlation between a given attitude and behavior, there is always the possibility that some other attitude that was not measured may be congruent with the behavior.

In the context of this discussion, one may fruitfully raise again Blumer's (1955) criticism. The state of present attitude theory is such that there are no rigorous criteria available for ascertaining when we are dealing with one attitude or with more than one attitude. Carlson (1956), for example, speaks of *an* attitude toward "Negroes moving into white neighborhoods." If this is *an* attitude, then there must be literally hundreds (perhaps thousands) of attitudes toward the Negro: attitudes toward Negroes "going to white schools," "swimming in white swimming pools," "white beaches," "white country clubs," and so forth. In such a case, the concept of attitude loses its conceptual power altogether and is indeed worth abandoning, as Blumer suggests. In line with the present conceptual definition of attitude as an organization of beliefs around an object or situation, however, it seems more appropriate to say that the way we feel about "Negroes moving into white neighborhoods" involves the activation of at least two attitudes that interact with one another; one concerns the Negro as an attitude object, the other concerns the white's everyday activity of living in his neighborhood.

FUNCTIONS OF AN ATTITUDE

Does an attitude possess drive-producing properties or do motives come from sources other than the attitude itself? This issue has provoked much debate in the literature and for lack of space will not be discussed here except to say that the controversy does not seem to have led to any empirical research. It is at present a moot point, as Chein (1948) points out.

In the past few decades there has, nevertheless, been a slow but steady advance toward more comprehensive formulations of the functions of an attitude. Beginning with Freud (1930) and followed by such thinkers as Lasswell (1930), Fromm (1941), Maslow (1943), and culminating in *The Authoritarian Personality* (Adorno, *et al.,* 1950), the proposition that attitudes serve mainly irrational, ego-defensive functions became widely accepted. Students of personality and culture and of sociology further emphasized the adjustive function of attitudes—the adjustment of primitive and modern man to their specific cultures and subcultures. Under the influence of these ideas, as well as of Gestalt psychology and more recent developments in psychoanalytic ego psychology that stressed the autonomous nature of an ego freed from the service of id and superego, Sarnoff and Katz (1954) and Smith, Bruner, and White (1956) were among the first to recognize explicitly the positive functions that attitudes also serve. This was shortly followed by several additional refinements leading to Katz's most recent formulation (1960, p. 170) of the four functions of an attitude:

1. *The instrumental, adjustive, or utilitarian function* upon which Jeremy Bentham and the utilitarians constructed their model of man. A modern expression of this approach can be found in behavioristic learning theory.
2. *The ego-defensive function* in which the person protects himself from acknowledging the basic truths about himself or the harsh realities in his external world. Freudian psychology and neo-Freudian thinking have been preoccupied with this type of motivation and its outcomes.
3. *The value-expressive function* in which the individual derives satisfactions from expressing attitudes appropriate to his personal values and to his concept of himself. This function is central to doctrines of ego psychology which stress the importance of self-expression, self-development, and self-realization.
4. *The knowledge function* based upon the individual's need to give adequate structure to his universe. The search for meaning, the need to understand, the trend toward better organization of perceptions and beliefs to provide clarity and consistency for the individual, are other descriptions of this function. The development of principles about perceptual and cognitive structure has been the contribution of Gestalt psychology.

These four functions are not regarded as operating in isolation from one another. A particular attitude may simultaneously serve several or all of these functions. In describing the function of belief systems, Rokeach (1960, p. 400) speaks of the need to "understand the world insofar as possible, and to defend against it insofar as necessary." Maslow (1963) speaks of the simultaneous functions—the need to know and the fear of knowing.

There is no reason to assume, however, that Katz's four functions are unique to attitudes. These are also the functions of single beliefs (for example, belief in the existence of a Creator), and of organizations of beliefs broader than attitudes—variously referred to by such terms as ideology, belief system, *Weltanschauung,* philosophy of life.

While the conceptual isolation of these four functions is a distinct step forward, we have not yet advanced sufficiently in our theories and methods to determine by objective procedures precisely which functions a particular attitude serves for a particular person and to what degree. The objective assessment of function becomes even more formidable when it is recognized that a particular function may be judged present when viewed from an inside, phenomenological standpoint, but absent when viewed from an outside, objective standpoint. In my research with three chronic paranoid schizophrenics (1964) it was found that various delusional beliefs served not only last-ditch, ego-defensive functions, but also knowledge functions. Delusions represent a search for meaning, giving the person holding them the illusion of understanding even though they are grotesque, ego-defensive distortions of reality.

An attitude can be likened to a miniature theory in science, having similar functions and similar virtues and vices. An attitude, like a theory, is a frame of reference, saves time because it provides us a basis for induction and deduction, organizes knowledge, has implications for the real world, and changes in the face of new evidence. A theory, like an attitude, is a prejudgment; it may be selective and biased, it may support the status quo, it may arouse affect when challenged, and it may resist change in the face of new evidence. An attitude, in short, may act in varying degrees like a good theory or a bad theory, and depending on what kind of a theory an attitude acts like, may serve one function better than another.

A final point concerns the relation between the value-expressive function and the remaining three functions. Does not the knowledge function also refer to a person's central values concerning truth, understanding, and the search for meaning, and does it not also serve self-expression, self-development, and self-realization? In the same way, the adjustive function involves such values as security, achievement, competence, success, and loyalty to ingroup. The ego-

131

defensive function may be reflected in the excessive glorification of such phenomenologically perceived positive values as neatness and cleanliness, thrift, honor, chivalry, sexual and racial purity, or may be reflected in the excessive condemnation of such negative values as lust, intemperance, subversion, waste and extravagance, and racial mongrelization.

It is thus possible to conceive of the value-expressive function as superordinate to all other functions, and to suggest that all of a person's beliefs and attitudes may be in the service of, or instrumental to, the satisfaction of one and another preexisting, often conflicting, values—adjustive values, ego-defensive values, knowledge and other self-realizing values. "Speaking generally," Woodruff and DiVesta write, "an individual will try to promote all of his higher positive values as opportunity permits, but each value will have precedence over those below it in his pattern, when a conflict between values develops" (1948, p. 646).

The function that seems to be served by all the values within one's value system is the enhancement of what McDougall (1926) has aptly called the master of all sentiment, the sentiment of self-regard.

SUMMARY

To summarize this chapter, the following more extended definition of attitude is offered: An attitude is a relatively enduring organization of interrelated beliefs that describe, evaluate, and advocate action with respect to an object or situation, with each belief having cognitive, affective, and behavioral components. Each of these beliefs is a predisposition that, when suitably activated, results in some preferential response toward the attitude object or situation, or toward others who take a position with respect to the attitude object or situation, or toward the maintenance or preservation of the attitude itself. Since an attitude object must always be encountered within some situation about which we also have an attitude, a minimum condition for social behavior is the activation of at least two interacting attitudes, one concerning the attitude object and the other concerning the situation.

132

SIX

Attitude Change and Behavioral Change

Since World War II many experimental studies of opinion change, carried out within a variety of conceptual frameworks, have been designed to increase our theoretical understanding of the conditions under which men's minds and behavior may change. While the main *empirical* focus of these studies is on behavioral changes in the expression of opinion, their main *theoretical* concern is with the conditions facilitating and inhibiting change in underlying beliefs and attitudes. To what extent have these experimental studies actually advanced our theoretical understanding of processes leading to attitude and behavior change? And to what extent have they improved our understanding of the fundamental structure of underlying attitudes, the way attitudes are organized with respect to one another, and the way atti-

133

tude and attitude change may affect behavior?

To discuss these questions I should like to begin with certain considerations, not about attitude change, but about the nature of attitude, and about the relationship between attitude and behavior. In contemporary approaches to "attitude change" the accent seems to be on the understanding of "change" rather than on the understanding of "attitude"; that is, one may note an interest in attitude theory as such only insofar as that interest is necessary to formulate testable hypotheses about attitude change. This would be roughly equivalent to a physicist telling us he is interested in theories of "nuclear change" rather than "nuclear structure" in order to understand better how to change nuclear structures.

The point of view to be developed here will therefore differ somewhat from that expressed by Arthur R. Cohen who, in the preface to his book, *Attitude Change and Social Influence,* wrote: "This book does not take up the definition and conceptualization of attitude, but instead assumes that there is a commonly accepted core of meaning for the term 'attitude change'" (1964, p. xi). I shall show that the concept of "attitude change" can have no "commonly accepted core of meaning" apart from the concept of attitude—that, indeed, theory and research on the nature, determinants, and consequents of attitude formation and maintenance are prerequisite to and inseparable from theory and research on attitude change. "Before tackling the important problem of attitude change," Sherif, Sherif, and Nebergall have remarked, "we must have a clear notion of *what* it is that changes and *what* it is that is resistant to change" (1965, p. vi). I contend that any consideration of the relation between attitude change and behavioral change necessarily rests on a prior consideration of the relation between attitude and behavior.

ATTITUDE AND BEHAVIOR

For the purposes of this discussion let me offer the following coordinated definitions of attitude and attitude change. An *attitude,* as defined in the preceding chapter, is a relatively enduring organization of beliefs about an object or situation predisposing one to respond in some preferential manner. *Attitude change* would then be a change in predisposition,[1] the change being either a change in the organization or structure of beliefs or a change in the content of one or more of the beliefs entering into the attitude organization.[2]

Especially important for the major thesis to be developed in this chapter is that an attitude may be focused on either an object or a situation, and that behavior is always a function of at least these two types of attitudes (to be called A_o and A_s). These assumptions have at least two implications worth noting. First, a given attitude-toward-object, whenever activated, need not always be behaviorally manifested or expressed in the same way or to the same degree. Its expression will vary adaptively as the attitude activated by the situation varies, with attitude-toward-situation facilitating or inhibiting the expression of attitude-toward-object, and vice versa. Any attitude-toward-object has the inherent property of being differentially manifested *along a range of values*[3] rather than as a single value, depending on the situation within which the attitude object is encountered.[4] This same property is inherent in any attitude-to-

---

[1] A *predisposition* would be defined as a hypothetical state of the organism which, when activated by a stimulus, causes a person to respond selectively, affectively, or preferentially to the stimulus.

[2] With *attitude change* defined as a change in structure as well as in content it becomes immediately evident that virtually all contemporary theories of attitude change are typically concerned with changes in content (with changes in for-ness or against-ness on a posttest as compared with a pretest) and that they have virtually ignored the structural kinds of attitude change that might come about as a result of development, education, or therapy, which need not necessarily involve a change in content. For example, a person may change with respect to degree of differentiation, integration, and breadth of an attitude without changing the strength of his positive or negative feelings toward the object of attitude. Similarly, when a person changes from a literal to a figurative interpretation of the Bible a structural rather than a substantive change is implied—that is, he may not have changed in his positive feelings about the sacredness of the Bible.

[3] The notion of an attitude-toward-object being manifested along a range of values is not the same idea as that expressed by Sherif and his co-workers (1965) when they speak of latitudes of acceptance, noncommitment, and rejection.

[4] H. C. Kelman expresses a similar view: "The attitudes expressed by an individual may vary from situation to situation, depending on the requirements of the situation in which he finds himself and the motivations

135

ward-situation. Consequently, a significant change of opinion toward an object may indicate nothing more than that a given attitude-toward-object was activated, and thus behaviorally expressed, in two different situations, S_1 and S_2, activating, respectively, two different attitudes-toward-situation, A_{s_1} and A_{s_2}.

Second, in principle there is no difference between the verbal and the nonverbal expression of a given attitude. Every expression in behavior, verbal or nonverbal, must be a confounding and a compounding function of at least two underlying attitudes—A_o and A_s. Thus, any verbal expression of opinion, like any nonverbal behavior, is also a function of at least two attitudes—attitude-toward-object and attitude-toward-situation—and ascertaining the extent to which the opinion is a manifestation of one attitude or the other, or both, requires careful inference rather than careless assumption.

COGNITIVE INTERACTION BETWEEN TWO ATTITUDES

It is not enough merely to assert that social behavior is a function of two attitudes. To predict behavioral outcome requires a model about the manner in which the two attitudes will cognitively interact with one another. Such a model, the belief-congruence model, is described in Chapter Four. While this model was originally formulated to deal with various issues raised by the Osgood and Tannenbaum congruity model (1955), with only minor modification it can be more generally employed to predict the behavioral outcome of cognitive interaction between the two attitudes A_o and A_s.

By applying this model to the present context, we can conjecture that whenever a person encounters an attitude object within

---

which he brings into this situation. What the individual says will be determined at least in part by what he considers to be proper in this situation and consonant with group norms, and also by what he considers to be most conducive to the achievement of his personal goals . . . . The amount of discrepancy depends on the situational requirements, on the person's goals, on his relation to the group, and on some of his personal characteristics" (1958b, pp. 25–26).

some situation, two attitudes, A_o and A_s, are activated; further, a comparison of the relative importance of these two attitudes is also activated. The two attitudes are assumed to affect behavior in direct proportion to their perceived importance with respect to one another. The more important A_o is perceived to be with respect to A_s, the more will the behavioral outcome be a function of A_o; conversely, the more important A_s is perceived to be with respect to A_o, the more will the behavioral outcome be a function of A_s.

By substituting A_o and A_s for *characterization* (C) and *subject* (S) in Formula [1] in Chapter Four we obtain:

$$B_{os} = (w)\, A_o + (1 - w)\, A_s \qquad\qquad [3]$$

where B_{os} refers to the behavior toward an object-within-a-situation and where (w) and $(1 - w)$ refer to the perceived importance of A_o and A_s relative to one another in the context of encountering a given object in a specified situation.[5]

How can the relative importance of two attitudes be determined? One way is by strictly empirical means—for example, by the method of paired comparison or by a rating procedure which would enable us to determine (w) and $(1 - w)$. In this instance we would not be able to predict on purely theoretical grounds the behavioral outcome of cognitive interaction between two attitudes of varying importance because we would have no way of knowing in advance their importance relative to one another or the absolute degree of that importance. Fortunately, however, the comparison of relative importance of the two attitudes does not occur in a vacuum; it takes place within the general framework of one's total belief system, wherein all beliefs and attitudes are arranged along a central-peripheral dimension of importance (Chapters One and Two) and wherein, furthermore, the beliefs and attitudes activate values varying in position along one's value hierarchy (Chapter Seven). Thus the two attitudes, A_o and A_s, can be compared as if to determine

---

[5] To express the above as deviations from a zero-point Formula [3] then becomes:

$$d_{os} = w\, (d_{A_o}) + (1 - w)\, d_{A_o} \qquad\qquad [3a]$$

Formula [2] in Chapter Four, which is designed to handle overassimilation, can similarly be transformed by substituting A_o and A_s for C and S.

their relative position along this central-peripheral dimension or as if to determine which values in the value hierarchy are activated by the two attitudes. Such conceptualizations enable us to make at least some educated guesses about which of two attitudes is the more important.

The question may now be raised whether it is ever possible to obtain a behavioral measure of a given attitude-toward-object that is uncontaminated by interaction with attitude-toward-situation. The extent to which this is possible is a function of the extent to which the situation is a "neutral" one—that is, a situation carefully structured by the experimenter to activate a relatively unimportant attitude-toward-situation that is of relatively little influence in the context of its interaction with attitude-toward-object. Learning how to structure the test or interview situation so that it is neutral is, of course, a major objective of attitude and survey research methodology, but this is only a methodological ideal to strive for and is probably rarely achieved in practice.

ATTITUDE CHANGE AND BEHAVIORAL CHANGE

The proposition that behavior is always a function of two interacting attitudes has important and disturbing implications for theory and research on attitude change and behavioral change. If expressing an opinion is a form of behavior, then expressing a changed opinion is also a form of behavior; a changed opinion must also be a function of the two attitudes previously discussed—attitude-toward-object and attitude-toward-situation. Similarly, any change in nonverbal behavior is also a form of behavior, and hence must also be a function of the same two attitudes. The question therefore arises: When there is a change in opinion or behavior, how can we tell whether or not there has also been a change in attitude and, if so, *which* attitude?

Although a reasonably clear distinction can be made between an underlying attitude and an expression of opinion (or, if you will, between a covert and overt attitude, or between a private and public attitude), and between an underlying attitude change and an expressed opinion change, one may nevertheless observe in the ex-

138

perimental and theoretical literature a general tendency to use these concepts interchangeably and thereby to shift the discussion back and forth between "attitude" and "opinion," and between "opinion change" and "attitude change." It becomes difficult to tell whether one is dealing with phenomena involving attitude change, expressed opinion change, or both. Many writers have ridden roughshod over the distinction between attitude and expressed opinion by using the phrases "attitude change," "opinion change," "attitude *and* opinion change" and "attitude *or* opinion change" more or less arbitrarily and interchangeably in the context of a single discussion. In this way the impression is created that a significant change in the expression of an opinion also represents a change in underlying attitude. For example, Hovland opens his paper, "Reconciling Conflicting Results Derived from Experimental and Survey Studies of Attitude [sic] Change":

> Two quite different types of research design are characteristically used to study the modification of attitudes [sic] through communication. In the first type, the *experiment,* individuals are given a controlled exposure to a communication and the effects evaluated in terms of the amount of change in attitude or opinion [sic] produced (1959, p. 8).

Festinger opens his article entitled, "Behavioral Support for Opinion [sic] Change": "The last three decades have seen a steady and impressive growth in our knowledge concerning attitudes and opinions [sic]" (1964, p. 404). Both of these writers, like many others, then employ the concepts of "attitude" and "opinion" indiscriminately in carrying forward their discussions, which are usually discussions about how some empirical data involving a change in *expressed* opinion bear on some hypothesis or theory regarding a change in attitude.

As one tries to assimilate the growing experimental literature on opinion change, he becomes increasingly aware that this literature concerns primarily the conditions affecting change in the expression of opinion. But this literature, considered as a whole, does not seem to have much to say about the conditions leading to a change in the content or structure of underlying predispositions (or, as Doob [1947] would have it, of implicit responses) toward objects or toward situations.[6]

Theories of attitude change, with certain exceptions (for example, Kelman's work on processes of social influence [1958a], related work on the public-private variable and work on the "sleeper" effect, Cohen [1964]), seem to be generally unconcerned with whether an expressed opinion change does or does not represent an underlying attitude change. Indeed, the classical paradigm employed in experimental studies of opinion change—pretest, treatment, posttest—is not capable of telling us whether an expressed opinion change indicates an attitude change; it can only tell us whether an expression of opinion has or has not changed as a result of a particular experimental treatment. If the main theoretical concern of experimental studies on expressed opinion change is with the conditions leading to attitude change, then the classical paradigm is basically faulty and should be replaced with other or modified experimental designs (to be discussed later) more suited to deal with this issue. It is not possible to ascertain whether the posttest response is a manifestation of a change in original predisposition or a manifestation of an altogether different predisposition activated by the posttest situation per se.

A closely related point concerns the relationship among attitude change, expressed opinion change, and behavioral change. In his presidential address to Division 8 of the American Psychological Association, Leon Festinger (1964) expressed astonishment over the "absence of research, and of theoretical thinking, about the effect of attitude change on subsequent behavior" (p. 405). He could find only three empirical studies relevant to this problem and they all showed "the *absence* of a relationship between opinion change

---

[6] Brewster Smith expresses a similar view in the following: ". . . investigators and theorists alike have been entirely too cavalier in referring to 'attitude change' without specifying the *aspect* of attitude—belief, feeling, or action tendency—in which change is predicted and measured. It often seems as though any stray feature of opinion in which change can readily be produced will do for experimentation" (1968, in press).

. . . and resulting behavior" (p. 416). Festinger stressed in his closing remarks that we ought not to ignore this problem or simply assume "a relationship between attitude change and subsequent behavior. . . ." He concluded that "The problem needs concerted investigation" (p. 417). And Cohen (1964), in a similar vein, wrote: "Until experimental research demonstrates that attitude change has consequences for subsequent behavior, we cannot be certain that our procedures . . . do anything more than cause cognitive realignments" (p. 138). It should be noted, first, that we cannot even be certain whether the experimental procedures employed "cause cognitive realignments" and, second, that the absence of relationship noted by Festinger and Cohen is not between attitude change and subsequent behavior but between two forms of behavior —expressed opinion change and subsequent nonverbal behavioral change. My main point is that there would seem to be not one but two problems requiring "theoretical thinking" and "concerted investigation." First: Why is it so difficult to demonstrate a relationship between attitude change and behavioral change? And, second: Why is it so difficult to demonstrate a relationship between one form of behavioral change and another?

I propose that expressed opinion or behavioral change is always a function of at least two attitudes. This proposition only complicates our attempts to determine whether or not a particular change in expressed opinion or behavior represents a change in attitude. Because we have to contend with two types of underlying attitudes, we now have four possible determinants of a change in expressed opinion or behavior: (1) interaction between attitude-toward-object and attitude-toward-situation, neither of which has changed; (2) a change in only the attitude-toward-object; (3) a change in only the attitude-toward-situation; or (4) a change in both attitude-toward-object and attitude-toward-situation.

Changes in expressed opinion or behavior as a result of (2), (3), and (4) are more or less self-evident, but the first determinant of expressed opinion or behavioral change—the interaction between A_o and A_s, neither of which has changed—merits further consideration because it goes against the widely held assumption that behavioral and expressed opinion changes cannot take place without a preceding change in attitude; it has implications for experimentally oriented and personality oriented studies of attitude and behavioral change; and it may open up fresh possibilities for bringing about changes in expressed opinion and behavior that do not depend on antecedent attitude change.

Let us consider a variety of instances in which a change of expressed opinion or behavior may be observed and understood without positing a change in underlying attitude. First, there are those actions that represent public conformity or compliance without private acceptance. Kelman (1958a) has shown that a subject exposed to an authority who is in a position to reward and punish will display a change of opinion in the direction of authority's opinion, but this change of opinion is manifested only under conditions of surveillance by authority and not under conditions of nonsurveillance. The surveillance condition represents a situation, S_1, activating the attitude A_{s_1}. The nonsurveillance condition represents another situation, S_2, activating another attitude, A_{s_2}. A change in expression of opinion from conditions of nonsurveillance to surveillance can readily be accounted for without assuming a change in underlying attitude-to-ward-object. The first measure of opinion toward a specified object is the behavioral result of the interaction between A_o and A_{s_1}; the second measure is a result of the interaction of the same A_o but another attitude, A_{s_2}. The change of expressed opinion toward the specified attitude object can be best understood as a reflection of the two different situations, each activating a different attitude-toward-situation. There is no need to assume that any one of the activated attitudes—A_o or A_{s_1} or A_{s_2}—has undergone any change.

Not all instances of expressed opinion change unaccompanied by attitude change necessarily represent acts of public compliance or conformity. Consider, for example, expressed opinion changes brought about as a result of what Orne (1962) has called the "demand characteristics" of the experimental situation or what Rosenberg (1965) has called "evaluation apprehension." Both terms refer to methodologically unwanted situational variables that may or may not motivate compliant behavior, variables that exist during the posttest period and not during the pretest period, and that activate some attitude-toward-situation persisting beyond that activated by the experimental treatment as such. Changes in expressed opinion toward an object from pre- to posttest thus result because two different situations activated two different attitudes, A_{s_1}, and A_{s_2}; we can therefore account for such changes without adding further assumptions regarding underlying attitude change.

Incidentally, changes in expressed opinion thus obtained are difficult to interpret because they violate a basic principle of measurement theory, namely, that repeated measurements designed to assess the effects of some experimental variable should be obtained under constant test conditions. Unlike survey research methodology, experimental studies of opinion change employing the pretest, treatment, and posttest paradigm cannot by their very nature guarantee the required constancy of testing conditions. The posttest situation is bound to be psychologically different from the pretest situation, the former activating different attitudes from the latter. Moreover, a posttest situation following one experimental treatment is not necessarily comparable with another posttest situation following a different experimental treatment. Orne expresses a similar view when he writes: "It should be clear that demand characteristics cannot be eliminated from experiments; all experiments will have demand characteristics and these will always have some effect" (1962, p. 779). Nevertheless, the proposition that behavior is a function of A_o and A_s would, if valid, require us to assess the relative effects of A_o and A_s in the pretest and posttest situations separately, in order to determine the meaning of a given change in expressed opinion.

Not only do social-psychological experiments have demand characteristics, but all social situations have them. Demand characteristics "cannot be eliminated from experiments" because they cannot be eliminated from any situation. Our two-attitude theory of behavior recognizes the inevitability of demand characteristics inherent in all social situations and tries to take them into systematic account in formulating the relationship between attitudes and behavior and between attitude change and behavioral change.

143

Let me turn now to another illustration, this time not of an opinion change but of a change in behavior, real-life behavior that is different from what we would ordinarily expect, that does not necessarily involve an attitude change, and that does not necessarily represent an act of public compliance or conformity. This experiment was described in Chapter Three. Recall that it took place in the natural setting of the personnel offices of two state mental hospitals near Detroit, Michigan. Recall also that the subjects, 50 applicants for low-status jobs, had to select as work partners two out of four other "job applicants"—two whites and two Negroes, one white and one Negro agreeing and one white and one Negro disagreeing with the subject on job-related issues.

One might reasonably expect that of 50 persons applying for low-status jobs a substantial number would, under the conditions described, choose two partners of their own race, given the salience of racial attitudes in our culture. But the results (shown in Table 8 in Chapter Three) do not confirm the expectation that attitude-toward-race is at all important.

Only two subjects of the 50—4 per cent—chose attitude objects of the same race (Pattern 3, S + S −), considerably less than would be expected even on a purely chance basis. That similarity of race is not an important criterion of choice of work partners, either for the white or for the Negro subjects, is indicated further in that three more subjects—6 per cent—chose two work partners of the other race (Pattern 4, O + O −). It is clear that the most frequent basis of choice is not similarity of race but similarity of belief. Thirty of the 50 subjects—60 per cent—chose two work partners, one white and one Negro, both of whom agreed with the subject, as compared with only two subjects who chose on the basis of similarity of race.

Even though we have no direct pretest and posttest data showing that there had been an actual change of behavior in the particular individuals studied, I would nevertheless regard these data as illustrating an instance of behavioral change that is not preceded by attitude change. The choice of work partners is not what we would ordinarily expect from 50 lower-class persons looking for a job, given the harsh facts of social discrimination in contemporary

American culture. The data suggest that the observed absence of racial discrimination is a function of the subject's knowing the stand taken by a Negro or white on an important issue. Assuming that for at least some of these subjects there had been a change in behavior from discrimination on the basis of race to discrimination on the basis of belief, we are again not required to posit any changes in attitudes underlying that behavior (although such changes can come about subsequently, as dissonance theory suggests). We can more simply understand such behavior as arising from an interaction between two attitudes that are activated by an object encountered within a situation in which the activated attitude-toward-situation far outweighs in importance the activated attitude-toward-object.

As a final example of behavioral change occurring without underlying attitude change, let me discuss an as yet unpublished study by Jamias and Troldahl (1965). These investigators were studying differences in willingness to adopt new agricultural practices recommended by agricultural extension agents as a function of personality and social system. The frequency of adoption of recommended agricultural practices—the dependent variable—was measured by a series of questions, each designed to determine which of several alternative procedures the dairy farmer followed in the day-to-day management of his farm. On each question, one of the alternatives was the one recommended by agricultural extension agents. Personality differences in receptivity to new information were measured by the Dogmatism Scale, and social system differences in receptivity were determined by identifying two types of rural townships in Michigan, one type identified as high and the other as low in their "value for innovativeness." The two types of social systems were readily identified by agricultural extension agents on the basis of the generally positive or negative attitude of the people in the townships toward extension activities, size of attendance at extension meetings, and similar factors. The results are shown in Table 13.

Statistical analyses show a highly significant interaction between receptivity in the personality system and receptivity in the social system. In the social system having a low value for innovativeness, the correlation between scores on the Dogmatism Scale and

Table 13

*Mean Adoption Rate by High and Low Dogmatic Groups Living in
Social Systems High and Low in "Value for Innovativeness"*

	SOCIAL SYSTEM IN WHICH VALUE FOR INNOVATIVENESS IS	
	LOW	HIGH
Low dogmatism group	7.3	6.2
High dogmatism group	4.9	6.8
Correlation between dogmatism and adoption rate	− .40	− .09

adoption rate is −.40; in the social system having a high value for innovativeness, the correlation is −.09. Highly dogmatic persons (scoring above the median on a modified form of the Dogmatism Scale constructed by Troldahl and Powell [1965]) living in social systems having a high value for innovativeness more frequently adopt recommendations of agricultural extension agents than highly dogmatic persons living in social systems having a low value for innovativeness. Conversely, low dogmatic subjects, regardless of the social system in which they live, have a relatively high adoption rate for new practices recommended by agricultural experts.

Table 13 shows that behavioral changes in highly dogmatic persons are the result of compliance or identification with social norms, and behavioral changes in low dogmatic persons are the result of a generalized receptivity to new information, which is routinely internalized according to its intrinsic correctness and usefulness. Again, no change of underlying attitude need be postulated to account for behavioral change, either in the unreceptive highly dogmatic subjects or in the more receptive low dogmatic subjects. Thus, the results suggest that we can produce changes in the behavior of different individuals through knowledge of personality organization, that is, a knowledge of how a particular situation will activate different beliefs and attitudes in persons who vary in the structure of their belief systems.

146

In summary, I have tried to suggest that a behavioral change (and this includes an expressed opinion change) may be determined by a change in attitude-toward-object, or in attitude-toward-situation, or both, or neither. I have concentrated mainly on behavioral changes that do not involve any kind of underlying attitude change, and have cited various instances of behavioral change in real life and in the laboratory that are attributable to compliance, demand characteristics, evaluation apprehension, the activation of salient beliefs and attitudes within the context of ongoing activity, or the activation of different beliefs and attitudes in persons with differing personality structures. All the illustrations cited have, I believe, a common thread. They all involve expressed opinion or behavioral changes that can be analyzed and reduced to two component attitudes, A_o and A_s, interacting within a figure-ground relationship, carrying differential weights, and affecting a behavioral outcome in proportion to their relative importance with respect to one another. These examples suggest that many kinds of behavioral change can be brought about by learning which attitude object to combine with which situation, which attitudes are activated by attitude object and situation in different personalities, and which outcome to expect from such interactions in different personalities.

Before terminating this portion of the discussion, however, let me mention one other relevant consideration that has thus far been altogether overlooked in contemporary theory and research on attitude change. If expressed opinion changes may be observed when there has been no underlying attitude change, then the converse is also true: an absence of expressed opinion change may be observed even after a change in underlying attitude has already taken place. For example, a dutiful son may continue to express proreligious sentiments even after he has changed his underlying attitudes toward religion, in order not to hurt his parents; a disillusioned Communist may continue to engage in Party activities because he is afraid of social ostracism; a person may continue to say "I love you" even after he has stopped loving. All these examples suggest a possible constancy in expressing an opinion despite a

147

change in attitude. The conditions under which such phenomena will occur deserve more study than they have received so far.

METHODS FOR ASSESSING ATTITUDE CHANGE

Thus far, I have tried merely to suggest that a change in behavior or expressed opinion may arise in different ways, and may or may not involve a change in underlying attitude-toward-object or attitude-toward-situation. I have also tried to suggest that the classical paradigm employed in experimental studies of opinion change cannot yield information about attitude change as such. The question is, then, how should we proceed if we wish to ascertain whether a given attitude has undergone change, or if we wish to increase the probability of correctly inferring that a given expressed opinion change represents an attitude change? I should like to discuss three methods, illustrating each with relevant research studies.

TEST FOR OPINION CHANGE ACROSS DIFFERENT SITUATIONS

If verbal or nonverbal behavior toward an object is observed in only one situation following an experimental treatment, we hardly have a basis for inferring a change of attitude. Orne (1962, p. 779) has pointed out: "If a test is given twice with some intervening treatment, even the dullest college student is aware that some change is expected, particularly if the test is in some obvious way related to the treatment." But the more posttest situations in which a changed opinion is manifested, the more confident we may be that a change in attitude has actually taken place. Any experimental study of expressed opinion change, if it is to qualify as a study in attitude change, should demonstrate the existence of change in at least two reasonably different situations.

One research design in which there are several posttests of opinion change is Kelman's study of three processes of social influence. Opinion change was assessed in three different posttest situations, under conditions of surveillance and salience, nonsurveillance and salience, and nonsurveillance and nonsalience. In the last condition, the posttest was administered "one or two weeks after the communication session, in a different place, under different auspices, and by a different experimenter" (1958a, p. 56). Kelman has shown that subjects who were given the experimental treatment designed to favor compliance manifested an opinion change only under conditions of surveillance and salience, thereby suggesting that there was no change in underlying attitude. Subjects who were given the internalization treatment, however, manifested opinion changes in all three posttest situations.

Another illustration of repeated posttest is my study on *The Three Christs of Ypsilanti,* which is concerned with underlying changes in delusional attitudes and beliefs among three paranoid schizophrenic patients who believed they were Jesus Christ. After several months of confrontation with each other over who was the real Christ, the youngest of the three, Leon Gabor, announced one day that he was no longer married to the Virgin Mary. Our problem was to determine whether or not this change in expressed opinion represented an underlying change in delusional belief. Our confidence that it did indeed represent such a delusional change increased as Leon Gabor repeatedly told us during the next few weeks and months in various contexts that he was about to get divorced, then that he was divorced, then that he had a new brother, then that his brother had married the Virgin Mary, then that he himself was about to remarry, then that he had remarried another woman, and so forth. Had we relied only on one "posttest" expression of a changed opinion about whom Leon was married to, our claim of a change in delusion would have been extremely weak.

A final illustration of repeated posttest is described in Chapter Seven. The experimental treatment described therein was designed to arouse inconsistent relations between two values, and between a value and an attitude. To find out if the experimental groups had changed their underlying values and attitudes as a result of the experimental treatment, the subjects were retested three weeks later and three to five months later. Three weeks later they were retested in the same classroom; three to five months later they were retested in their residence halls, no longer under the watchful eye of the experimenters, mailing the questionnaires back when

149

finished. The fact that value and attitude changes were observed on both occasions and the fact that the changes observed on the second posttest were often larger than those observed on the first posttest increase our confidence that the significant changes obtained do indeed represent changes in underlying values and attitudes.

In the experimental literature on opinion change, one may find an occasional study in which two or more posttest situations are employed, but, unless I am mistaken, such studies are the exception rather than the rule. In the typical experiment the posttest is given only once, usually within a short time after the experimental treatment; thus the meaning of the expressed opinion change in relation to attitude change is highly equivocal.

The preceding remarks concern the assessment of change in underlying attitudes-toward-object in several posttest situations. I have not said anything about assessing change in underlying attitude-toward-situation because this type of attitude is typically not employed in experimental studies of attitude change. The principle would seem to be the same: instead of testing for change in opinion toward an attitude object across situations, a change in attitude-toward-situation would be tested by substituting various attitude objects that might be encountered within that situation.

TEST FOR CHANGES OF SEVERAL OPINIONS IN ONE SITUATION

In the classical paradigm only one opinion is pretested, experimentally treated, and then posttested. Evaluation of the nature of the opinion change is difficult because the expressed opinion is compared only with itself. But suppose several opinions that are thought to be systematically related to one another in some way were pretested, experimentally treated, and then assessed for change all in one posttest situation? Suppose, further, that we find differential opinion changes and that these differential changes are systematically related to one another in the same way as the original opinions are related to one another?

A good illustration of differential opinion changes observed in one situation is the Rokeach, Reyher, and Wiseman experiment described in Chapter Two, wherein 55 beliefs ranging from central beliefs about self-identity to inconsequential beliefs were subjected to change through hypnotic induction. This experimental situation, it will be recalled, was designed to determine whether different kinds of beliefs ranging systematically along a theoretically postulated central-peripheral dimension can be changed through hypnosis and, if so, which kinds of beliefs will be the easiest to change and which the most difficult. In other words, we were interested in determining whether differential changes in several beliefs will occur as a result of a single experimental treatment.

The various results described in Chapter Two show that the hypothesized differential changes in expressed opinions were indeed obtained as a result of one experimental treatment. As expected, the amount of change varied in inverse proportion to centrality of belief, the primitive beliefs changing least as a result of hypnotic suggestion, authority beliefs changing more, peripheral beliefs changing still more, and inconsequential beliefs changing the most. I might add that these differential results were obtained on three occasions: immediately after the hypnotic suggestion, a short time later while the subject was still under hypnosis, and immediately after he was awakened. It would be difficult to attribute such differential changes to compliance or to the operation of any other posttest situational variable, because the posttest situation, and the attitude activated by that situation, was a constant. Yet opinion changes varied systematically in the same way the original opinions varied, namely, as a function of centrality-peripherality. To account for such differential changes we would have to infer that they are manifestations of differential changes in underlying attitudes.

Another illustration from our own research program where several opinion changes are obtained in one posttest situation may again be taken from *The Three Christs* study. As a result of experimental confrontation with others over the issue of who was the real Christ, Leon Gabor reported that he had changed his name from *Dr. Domino Dominorum et Rex Rexarum, Simplis Christianus Pueris Mentalis Doktor, the reincarnation of Jesus Christ of Nazareth* to Dr. R. I. Dung. Again the problem was whether this expressed opinion change regarding a new identity represented a true

151

underlying change. And, again, our confidence increased that it did indeed represent a true change when he expressed a network of additional differential changes in opinion that were wholly consistent with the expressed change of name.

The value change study described in Chapter Seven provides us with a final illustration of differential change. The experimental manipulation of two target values—*freedom* and *equality*—led to differential increases and decreases in yet other values and attitudes within the subjects' value-attitude systems.

TEST FOR OTHER BEHAVIORAL CHANGES ACCOMPANYING A GIVEN OPINION CHANGE

If a single expressed opinion change truly represents a change in underlying attitude, it is reasonable to expect that such a change will be accompanied by other changes—cognitive, affective, or behavioral—that theoretically should be related to the change in attitude. It is difficult to believe that a change in expressed opinion representing a true change in attitude would have no other behavioral manifestations. That Festinger and Cohen find virtually no studies in the experimental literature showing behavioral change following an attitude change only serves to reinforce my suspicion that most current experimental studies on opinion change do not deal with true attitude change, but with superficial opinion changes.

I should like to draw attention to some data, again from our own research program, which illustrate that behavioral changes following or accompanying opinion changes can indeed be obtained. In *The Three Christs* study, one may note many changes in Leon Gabor's behavior following changes in expressed opinion. After he verbally claimed to have a new wife, Madame Yeti Woman, his behavior with respect to money changed. He accepted, handled, and spent money when it allegedly came from Madame Yeti; these were actions we had never before observed. Furthermore, Leon Gabor, following suggestions allegedly coming from his new wife, changed the song with which he always opened the meetings on days he was chairman from *America* to *Onward Christian Soldiers,*

152

a permanent behavioral change. Again, these behavioral changes serve to increase our confidence in the inference that Leon's expressed opinion change represented a true change in underlying delusion.

Perhaps more impressive in this respect is a study of changes in expressed values by Kemp (1960). His subjects were all religiously minded persons enrolled in a special training curriculum designed to prepare them for positions as Boy Scout executives or YMCA or YWCA secretaries. Kemp was interested in determining whether changes in values and in behavior were a function of personality. The subjects were given the Allport-Vernon Scale of Values while still in college in 1950. Six years later they were contacted again, given the Dogmatism Scale, and retested with the Allport-Vernon Scale. As shown in Table 14, closed, middle, and open-minded subjects all expressed identical value patterns in 1950, but in 1956, the rank order of values remained the same only for the middle group, and had changed for the closed and open groups:

Although *religious* values were still predominant in all groups, the closed group increased in *political* and *economic* values and decreased markedly in *social* values. The open group remained unchanged in its *religious* and *social* values but increased in *theoretical* values and decreased in *economic* and *political* values. . . . The vocational choices . . . follow closely these changes or non-changes in value patterns. Roughly 70 per cent of the middle group became Boy Scout executives as planned, or entered closely related professions. But most of the open and closed subjects changed their vocational choice after leaving college; the open subjects more frequently entered vocations requiring more advanced professional training in careers involving social welfare, and the closed subjects more frequently entered military and commercial careers of an administrative nature (pp. 345–346).

That vocational changes accompanied changes in scores on the Allport-Vernon Scale of Value strengthens the likelihood that the changes in expressed values represent real changes in underlying values.

153

Table 14

Rank Order of Importance of Six Values for the Total Group and for
Open, Middle, and Closed Subgroups in 1950 and 1956

	(N)	RELIGIOUS	SOCIAL	POLITICAL	ECONOMIC	THEORETICAL	AESTHETIC
Test 1950:							
Open	(25)	1	2	3	4	5	6
Middle	(54)	1	2	3	4	5	6
Closed	(25)	1	2	3	4	5	6
Total group	(104)	1	2	3	4	5	6
Retest 1956:							
Open	(25)	1	2	4	6	3	5
Middle	(54)	1	2	3	4	5	6
Closed	(25)	1	5	2	3	4	6
Total group	(104)	1	2.5	2.5	5	4	6

Source: M. Rokeach, *The Open and Closed Mind*, New York, Basic Books, 1960, p. 339.

154

CONCLUSION

In closing, I should like to concede that the point of view I have presented will probably not appeal to those who, disliking to think in terms of genotypes and phenotypes, would insist on equating an attitude with its operational measurement by some opinion questionnaire. But, starting with a conception of attitude as a hypothetical construct, I have proposed that the literature on opinion change does indeed tell us a good deal about the social influence variables and cognitive processes affecting changes in expressed opinion. However, this is a literature concerning changes which, in the main, seem to be localized in the region of the lips and do not seem to affect the mind and heart, nor the hands and feet. It is a literature which, in the main, concerns phenotypic changes in opinion that cannot necessarily be taken as indications of, or be equated with, genotypic changes in attitude. It is a literature which, in the main, seems concerned with momentary modifications in the expression of opinions and not with enduring changes of beliefs, attitudes, or values.

The view developed here on the relations existing among attitude, attitude change, and behavioral change is incomplete, however. It has neglected other kinds of change that must sooner or later be considered if there is to be a truly systematic consideration of antecedents and consequents of attitude and behavioral change, namely, the problem of changes in values, in ideology, in total belief systems, in therapy, and in personality. It seems to me that contemporary theory and research on opinion change, dealing as they typically do with changes in single and isolated expressions of opinion, and selecting as they typically do opinions that are, as Hovland (1959) points out, "relatively uninvolving" and thus easily capable of manipulation within the context of a relatively brief experimental session, have somehow lost touch with broader issues. I hope that the analysis presented in this chapter will serve as a contribution toward our regaining contact with these broader and more significant kinds of change, which may affect and be affected by our everyday life in local, national, and international affairs.

SEVEN

Organization and Change within Value-Attitude Systems

This chapter presents a first report of an ongoing research program broadly concerned with the relations existing among values, attitudes, and behavior.[1] In the first part of this chapter I consider the functional and structural role that attitudes, values, and value systems play within a person's total system of belief, some conditions that might lead to enduring change in values, and some consequences that might be expected to follow from such change. In the second part of this chapter I describe our approach to the measurement of values and value systems, and report some results relevant to

[1] I would like to express my appreciation to Charles Hollen, Robert Beech, and Joseph Bivins for their contributions to the research reported herein.

156

several facets of the theoretical formulations discussed in the first part of the chapter.

Unlike other cognitive approaches in contemporary social psychology which focus attention on attitude organization and change, we are focusing our attention primarily on value organization and change. This shift of focus from attitude to value evolves from certain second thoughts that I would like to share with you about the central position the attitude concept has held in social psychology.

It is now exactly half a century since Thomas and Znaniecki (1918) first proposed that the study of social attitudes should be the central problem of social psychology. In the intervening years the attitude concept has indeed occupied a dominant place in theory and research, and it has been assigned prominent space in the textbooks and handbooks of social psychology. "The concept of attitude," Allport has written in one of these handbooks, "is probably the most distinctive and indispensable concept in contemporary American psychology. No other term appears more frequently in experimental and theoretical literature" (1935, p. 798).

Now, half a century later, the time is perhaps ripe to ask whether the attitude concept should continue to occupy the central position it has enjoyed for so long. In raising this question, I do not mean to suggest that it is no longer important or that it is less important now than in the past, but only to ask whether there is now, and indeed whether there always has been, an even more deserving candidate for this central position.

Several considerations lead me to place the value concept in nomination ahead of the attitude concept. First, value seems to be a more dynamic concept since it has a strong motivational component as well as cognitive, affective, and behavioral components. Second, while attitude and value are both widely assumed to be determinants of social behavior, value is a determinant of attitude as well as of behavior. Third, if we further assume that a person possesses considerably fewer values than attitudes, then the value concept provides us with a more economical analytic tool for de-

157

scribing and explaining similarities and differences between persons, groups, nations, and cultures.

Consider, finally, the relative ubiquitousness of the value and attitude concepts across disciplines. While attitudes seem to be a specialized concern mainly of psychology and sociology, values have long been a center of theoretical attention across many disciplines—philosophy, education, political science, economics, anthropology, and theology, as well as psychology and sociology. All these disciplines share a common concern with the antecedents and consequents of value organization and value change. Around such a shared concern we may more realistically anticipate genuine interdisciplinary collaboration.

It may seem somewhat paradoxical, in view of the more central theoretical status generally accorded the value concept, that we should have witnessed over the years a more rapid theoretical advance in the study of attitude rather than of value. One reason for this, I suspect, was the more rapid development of methods for measuring attitudes, due to the efforts of such men as Bogardus, Thurstone, Likert, and Guttman. A second reason, perhaps, was the existence of a better consensus on the meaning of attitude than of value. A third possible reason is that attitudes were believed to be more amenable to experimental manipulation than values. In any event, the ready availability of quantitative methods for measuring attitudes made it only a matter of time before experimentally minded social psychologists sought to determine whether the attitude variable could be fruitfully fitted into the classical pretest-treatment-posttest paradigm. After finding that attitudes were indeed susceptible to experimental influence, a demand was created for theories of attitude organization and change to explain the results, rather than for theories of value organization and change.

I should like to draw special attention to one consequence of the fact that it was the attitude rather than the value variable which thus came into the experimentalist's focus. Bypassing the problem of values and their relation to attitudes, we settled perhaps a bit too hastily for studies that I shall call problems of persuasion

158

to the neglect of what I shall call problems of education and re-education. We emphasized the persuasive effects of group pressure, prestige, order of communication, role playing, and forced compliance on attitudes, but we neglected the more difficult study of the more enduring effects of socialization, educational innovation, psychotherapy, and cultural change on values.

It was, therefore, our hope that in shifting from a concern with attitudes to a concern with values we would be dealing with a concept that is more central, more dynamic, more economical, a concept that would invite a more enthusiastic interdisciplinary collaboration, and that would broaden the range of the social psychologist's traditional concern to include problems of education and reeducation as well as problems of persuasion.

DEFINITIONS OF ATTITUDES, VALUES, AND VALUE SYSTEMS

The discussion thus far has proceeded on the assumption that the conceptual boundaries between an attitude and a value, and between a value and a value system, are clear and widely understood. This assumption is surely unwarranted. Since I plan to employ these concepts in distinctively different ways, I must first define them and then try to point out the main distinctions among them.

An attitude, as already stated in Chapter Five, is an organization of several beliefs focused on a specific object (physical or social, concrete or abstract) or situation, predisposing one to respond in some preferential manner. Some of these beliefs about an object or situation concern matters of fact and others concern matters of evaluation. An attitude is thus a package of beliefs consisting of interconnected assertions to the effect that certain things about a specific object or situation are true or false, and other things about it are desirable or undesirable.

Values, on the other hand, have to do with modes of conduct and end-states of existence. To say that a person "has a value"

159

is to say that he has an enduring belief that a specific mode of conduct or end-state of existence is personally and socially preferable to alternative modes of conduct or end-states of existence. Once a value is internalized it becomes, consciously or unconsciously, a standard or criterion for guiding action, for developing and maintaining attitudes toward relevant objects and situations, for justifying one's own and others' actions and attitudes, for morally judging self and others, and for comparing self with others. Finally, a value is a standard employed to influence the values, attitudes, and actions of at least some others—our children's, for example.

This definition of value is highly compatible with those advanced by Clyde Kluckhohn (1951), Brewster Smith (1963), and Robin Williams (1967). So defined, values differ from attitudes in several important respects. While an attitude represents several beliefs focused on a specific object or situation, a value is a single belief that transcendentally guides actions and judgments across specific objects and situations, and beyond immediate goals to more ultimate end-states of existence. Moreover, a value, unlike an attitude, is an imperative to action, not only a belief about the preferable but also a preference for the preferable (Lovejoy, 1950). Finally, a value, unlike an attitude, is a standard or yardstick to guide actions, attitudes, comparisons, evaluations, and justifications of self and others.

The distinction between preferable modes of conduct and preferable end-states of existence is a more or less familiar one in the philosophical literature on values: it is a distinction between values representing means and ends, between instrumental and terminal values (Lovejoy, 1950; Hilliard, 1950). An instrumental value is therefore defined as a single belief that always takes the following form: "I believe that such-and-such a mode of conduct (for example, honesty, courage) is personally and socially preferable in all situations with respect to all objects." A terminal value takes a comparable form: "I believe that such-and-such an end-state of existence (for example, salvation, a world at peace) is personally and socially worth striving for." Only those words or phrases that can be meaningfully inserted into the first sentence are instrumental values, and only those words or phrases that can be meaningfully inserted into the second sentence are terminal values.

Consider next the concept of value system. Many writers have observed that values are organized into hierarchical structures and substructures. Operationally speaking, the concept of value system suggests a rank-ordering of values along a continuum of importance. And given the distinction I have just drawn between instrumental and terminal values, two separate value systems may be posited—instrumental and terminal—each with a rank-ordered structure of its own, each, no doubt, functionally and cognitively connected with the other, and both systems connected with many attitudes toward specific objects and situations.

Often a person is confronted with a situation in which he cannot behave in a manner congruent with all of his values. The situation may activate two or more values in conflict with one another. For example, a person may have to choose between behaving compassionately or behaving competently, but not both; between behaving truthfully or patriotically, but not both. Similarly, in a given situation a person may have to choose between such terminal values as self-fulfillment and prestige, between salvation and a comfortable life. A person's value system may thus be said to represent a learned organization of rules for making choices and for resolving conflicts—between two or more modes of behavior or between two or more end-states of existence.

Given a reasonably sizable number of values to be arranged in a hierarchy, a large number of variations are theoretically possible, but it is extremely unlikely that all such value patterns will actually be found. Many social factors can be expected to restrict sharply the number of obtained variations. Similarities of culture, social system, caste and class, sex, occupation, education, religious up-bringing, and political orientation are major variables that are likely to shape in more or less similar ways the value systems of large numbers of people. We may thus expect that while personality factors will give rise to variations in individual value systems, cultural, institutional, and social factors will nevertheless restrict such variations to a reasonably small number of dimensions.

161

MENTAL ORGANIZATION OF VALUE-ATTITUDE SYSTEMS

The conceptual distinctions I have drawn between attitudes and values, between instrumental and terminal values, and between values and value systems suggest that there are different numbers of attitudes, instrumental values, and terminal values within a person's total system of beliefs. The distinctions suggest that an adult possesses thousands and perhaps tens of thousands of attitudes toward specific objects and situations, but only several dozens of instrumental values and perhaps only a few handfuls of terminal values. Such a difference in numbers immediately points to the presence of a hierarchically connected system of attitudes and values. Let us suppose that the thousands of attitudes within a person's belief system are all in the service of and cognitively connected with perhaps a few dozen instrumental values, and that the instrumental values are, in their turn, functionally and cognitively connected with an even fewer number of terminal values.[2] We can further suppose that this value-attitude system is more or less internally consistent and will determine behavior, and that a change in any part of the system will affect other connected parts and lead to behavioral change.

It is now possible to discern the outlines of at least four separate subsystems within the value-attitude system just described, and we may concern ourselves with problems of measurement, organization, and change within any one of these subsystems considered separately. First, several beliefs may be organized together to form a

[2] Woodruff and DiVesta (1948) were perhaps the first to formulate clearly the idea that attitudes are functionally and cognitively connected with values. The kinds of values these authors and others (Smith, 1949; Peak, 1955; Rosenberg, 1956; and Carlson, 1956) apparently had in mind were terminal values. Scott (1959, 1965), on the other hand, apparently had instrumental values in mind. The present formulation attempts to go beyond these formulations to propose an operational distinction between terminal and instrumental values, to propose that there are many attitudes, fewer instrumental values, and even fewer terminal values, and to propose that attitudes, instrumental and terminal values are all functionally interrelated.

162

single attitude focused on a specific object or situation. Second, two or more attitudes may be organized together to form a larger attitudinal system, say, a religious or political ideology. Third and fourth, two or more values may be organized together to form an instrumental or a terminal value system.[3]

This description of a person's value-attitude system is incomplete, however, unless we also represent within it at least three additional kinds of cognitions or beliefs that are continually fed into the value-attitude system, in order to provide it with the raw materials for growth and change. Coordinated with the four subsystems just mentioned there are, fifth, the cognitions a person may have about his own behavior (or commitments to behavior); sixth, the cognitions he may have about the attitudes, values, motives, and behavior of significant others; and seventh, the cognitions he may have about the behavior of physical objects. All such cognitions may be experienced by a person as being consistent or inconsistent to varying degrees with one another or with one or more of the attitudes or values within his value-attitude system.

VALUES, ATTITUDES, AND BEHAVIOR

In Chapters Five and Six a "two-attitude theory of behavior" was proposed: Behavior with respect to an object is always a function of at least two attitudes—attitude toward object and atti-

---

[3] As already indicated, the major portion of our combined research efforts has been directed primarily toward measuring and gaining a better understanding of organization and change in the first and second subsystems of the more inclusive value-attitude system—the single and multiple attitude organizations. But what seems to have received considerably less systematic attention thus far are problems of measurement, organization, and change that are directly focused on the third and fourth subsystems as such—the instrumental and terminal value systems—and problems of organization and change in the more inclusive value-attitude system containing all four subsystems. Nevertheless, a number of studies have moved significantly in this direction. In addition to the studies already cited the following are especially relevant: the study of terminal value patterns by Hunt (1935), Smith's work on value as a determinant of attitude (1949), White's approach to value analysis (1951), Morris' formulation of 13 Ways (1956), and Kluckhohn and Strodtbeck's cross-cultural study of value orientations (1961).

tude toward the situation within which the object is encountered. Moreover, A_o and A_s will cognitively interact and behavior will therefore be a function of the relative importance of A_o and A_s in the context of their interaction.

This "two-attitude theory" can now be elaborated to take into account the relationships existing between values and attitudes and the role that values as well as attitudes might play in determining social behavior. Whenever a social object is encountered within a social situation it activates two attitudes, A_o and A_s. Each of these two attitudes activates, in turn, a subset of instrumental and terminal values with which it is functionally connected. Behavior toward a social object within a social situation will therefore be a function of the relative importance of the two activated attitudes, A_o and A_s which, in turn, will be a function of the number and the relative importance of all the instrumental and terminal values activated by A_o as compared with all the instrumental and terminal values activated by A_s.

CHANGE IN VALUE-ATTITUDE SYSTEMS

We not only seek to describe the manner in which value-attitude systems may be organized but also how they may change. In common with other balance formulations the present theory also postulates a motivation for consistency, but consistency is defined, primarily, as consistency with self-esteem (Deutsch, Krauss, and Rosenau, 1962; Malewski, 1962; Frentzel, 1965) and, secondarily, as consistency with logic or reality. While a person will typically strive for both kinds of consistency, consistency with self-esteem is probably a more compelling consideration than consistency with logic or reality.

However, we seek to go beyond contemporary consistency theories to seek out systematically all the combinations of elements or subsystems of elements that can conceivably be brought into an inconsistent relation with one another. In our efforts to formulate a theory of organization and change within value-attitude systems we are groping toward a theory of dissonance-induction as well as a theory of dissonance-reduction. We ask: How many different types of inconsistent relations might a person experience naturally, or might he be induced to so experience? Are there theoretical grounds for supposing that certain types of inconsistent relations are more likely to be psychologically upsetting than other types? Will certain types of inconsistent relations lead to larger and more enduring change than other types? And are certain types of inconsistent relations likely to have more far-reaching consequences for cognition and behavior than other types?

Let us posit that a person strives for consistency within and between each and every one of the seven subsystems that I have just represented within the value-attitude system. If we label these subsystems A to G then we can produce a matrix, shown in Table 15, of all the possible relations a person might experience or might be induced to experience as inconsistent. The matrix suggests at

Table 15

Matrix of Inconsistent Relations
Possible within the Value-Attitude System

COGNITIVE ORGANIZATION OF	A	B	C	D	E	F	G
A. Attitude	X^1	x	x	x^2	x^3	x^4	x
B. Attitude system		X^5	x	x	x	x^6	x
C. Instrumental value system			X	x	x	x	x
D. Terminal value system				X	x	x	x
E. Cognitions about own behavior					X	x	x
F. Cognitions about significant others' attitudes, values, motives, or behavior						X	x
G. Cognitions about behavior of nonsocial objects							X

[1] McGuire (1960).
[2] Abelson and Rosenberg (1958).
[3] Festinger (1957) and Brehm and Cohen (1962).
[4] Sherif (1965), Yale group (1953, 1957, 1959), and McGuire (1964).
[5] Osgood and Tannenbaum (1955).
[6] Heider (1958) and Newcomb (1961).

least 28 relations that may be experienced as cognitively inconsistent. The diagonals represent seven such possibilities *within* each of the subsystems: AA represents an inconsistent relation between two or more beliefs within a single attitude organization; BB represents an inconsistent relation between two or more attitudes within an attitude system; CC represents an inconsistent relation between two or more instrumental values within the instrumental value system; and so on. The remaining 21 relations shown in Table 15 represent possible experiences of inconsistency *between* subsystems. Type CD, for example, represents an inconsistent relation between a terminal and instrumental value, as when a person discovers that he places a high value on salvation but a low value on forgiveness; Type AC represents an inconsistent relation between an instrumental value and an attitude, as when a person discovers that he places a high value on tenderness but favors escalating the Viet Nam war.

If we now scrutinize contemporary theories of balance and attitude change through the latticework of this matrix we may compare them with one another for comprehensiveness of formulation or extent of overlap. Osgood, for example, who is concerned with incongruities between any two attitudes linked together by an assertion, is apparently dealing with inconsistencies of Type BB; Festinger, who is typically concerned with inconsistencies between an attitude and a cognition about behavior, is apparently dealing with inconsistencies of Type AE. I have tried to locate within the matrix the specific types of inconsistencies with which various balance and attitude change theorists have been mainly concerned. Whether or not the reader agrees with my location of the several theories, the present analysis suggests that, considered all together, they are studying different parts of the same elephant, that they are concentrating on different kinds of inconsistent relations as represented within different cells of the matrix. The present analysis further suggests that a majority of all the possible experiences of consistency and inconsistency, especially those implicating the more central parts of the value-attitude system, still remain for the most part unexplored.

The intriguing question now before us is which of the 28

types of inconsistency are likely to lead to the greatest payoff in magnitude and enduringness of change, in their effects on other parts of the system, and in their effects on behavior. A look at the matrix suggests that the greatest payoff should result from bringing into an inconsistent relation the most central elements of the system, those conceived to have the most direct functional and structural connections with the rest of the system. Attention is thus drawn especially to Type DD in the matrix—an inconsistent relation between two or more terminal values—and close behind, to other relations combining D with A, B, C, E, F, or G. Since these terminal values are the most centrally located structures, having many connections with other parts of the system, we would expect inconsistencies that implicate such values to be emotionally upsetting and their effects to dissipate slowly, to be long-remembered, to endure over time, to lead to systematic changes in the rest of the value system, to lead to systematic changes in connected attitudes, and, finally, to culminate in behavior change.

I should like next to propose three main methods for inducing a state of inconsistency between any two of the elements shown in Table 15. The first two are well known, and the third is perhaps new. First, a person may be induced to engage in behavior that is inconsistent with his attitudes or values. Second, a person may be exposed to new information from a significant other that is inconsistent with information already represented within his value-attitude system. A third way, which to the best of my knowledge has not been employed thus far, and which I hope will open the door to an experimental study of problems of education and reeducation, is to expose the person to information about states of inconsistency already existing within his own value-attitude system. What I am proposing here is somewhat analogous to the effects that may be generated by showing a person undergoing a medical examination an X-ray of himself that reveals previously unsuspected and unwelcome medical information. It may be assumed that in every person's value-attitude system there already exist inherent contradictions of which he is unaware for one reason or another—compartmentalization due to ego-defense, conformity, intellectual limitations, or an

167

uncritical internalization of the contradictory values and attitudes of his reference groups. In other words, feelings of inconsistency may be induced not only by creating it but also by exposing to self-awareness inconsistencies already existing within the system below the threshold of awareness.[4]

SOME RESEARCH FINDINGS

I would now like to describe some findings from our current research program that bear on the theory of organization and change just presented. Our first problem was to find a way to measure value systems, and our approach to this problem was extremely simple. Initially, we collected a dozen instrumental values (for example, broadminded, clean, forgiving, responsible), another dozen terminal values (for example, a comfortable life, equality, freedom, salvation), alphabetized each set of values, and simply asked our subjects to rank-order them for importance. In a matter of a few minutes we were thus able to obtain data on the relative importance our subjects attached to 24 values—12 instrumental and 12 terminal.

It is not possible here to go into the details of how we initially selected these values and how we improved upon them in successive versions, or to discuss all the results we obtained. It is sufficient to say here that the rank-orderings of instrumental and terminal values seemed to be reasonably stable over time: Form A, our initial form composed of 12 instrumental and 12 terminal values, had test-retest

---

[4] Stotland, Katz, and Patchen (1959) have reported some incidental evidence that subjects whose attitude was at variance with their values were more likely to change their attitude in order to bring it into a consistent relation with their values. The functional approach of Katz and his co-workers is, however, somewhat different from the approach discussed here. First, the theoretical approach of these investigators, like that of others, is primarily focused on the problem of attitude change and not on value change. Second, they have approached the problem of attitude change by attempting to give their subjects insight into the psychodynamics of their attitudes. In contrast, the present approach skirts the problem of underlying psychodynamics and instead merely attempts to give the subjects insight into whether certain relations within their systems are or are not consistent.

reliabilities in the .60's after a seven-week period; Form D, our fourth and final version composed of 18 instrumental and 18 terminal values, had test-retest reliabilities in the .70's after seven weeks. In the course of developing these scales we obtained data on the similarities and differences in instrumental and terminal values of many groups differing in age, sex, education, occupation, religion, and politics. We also obtained data on the factorial dimensions along which instrumental and terminal values are organized, both separately and together; on the relation between instrumental and terminal values, between values and attitudes, and between values and behavior.[5]

Especially relevant to the validity of our approach to the theory and measurement of value systems are the results we obtained on the relation between values and behavior, and between values and attitudes. In this connection, let me cite some statistically significant findings concerning religious and political values. We found that the rank-ordering of one terminal value alone—*salvation*—highly predicts church attendance. College students who go to church "once a week or more" rank *salvation* first on the average among 12 terminal values, but other groups—those who attend church "once a month," "once a year," or "never"—typically rank *salvation* last among 12 terminal values.

Table 16 shows significant relationships between two distinctively political terminal values—*equality* and *freedom*—and attitude toward civil rights demonstrations. Those who report they are "sympathetic, and have participated" in civil rights demonstrations rank *freedom* first on the average and *equality* third among 12 terminal values; those who are "sympathetic, but have not participated" rank *freedom* first and *equality* sixth; and those who are "unsympathetic" rank *freedom* second and *equality* eleventh.

A second kind of data we are collecting has a purely descriptive purpose, to determine the extent to which fundamental similarities and differences among various groupings can be mean-

---

[5] A fuller report on these data will be presented in a future publication.

169

Table 16

*Composite Rank-Order for Freedom and Equality
and Attitude toward Civil Rights Demonstrations**

	YES, AND HAVE PARTICIPATED $N = 10$	YES, BUT HAVE NOT PARTICIPATED $N = 320$	NO, NOT SYMPATHETIC $N = 114$	p†
Freedom	1	1	2	.01
Equality	3	6	11	.001

* All cell entries are based on the rank-ordering of median scores obtained for 12 terminal values. All references in the remainder of this paper to "composite rank order" are similarly defined.

† Obtained by Kruskal-Wallis one-way analysis of variance (Siegel, 1956).

ingfully and economically described solely in value terms. Some of these descriptive data were predictable in advance on the basis of various considerations, thus providing us with additional validity data. For example, *salvation* ranked first among 12 terminal values by Lutheran ministers, by students attending a Calvinist college, and by Catholic and Lutheran students attending a midwestern university, but was typically ranked last by Jewish students and by those expressing no religious preference.

Our descriptive data, however, also provide us with many surprises that cannot be altogether predicted in advance. Consider, for example, some contrasting patterns of findings on *freedom* and *equality* shown in Table 17. Fifty policemen from a medium-sized

Table 17

*Composite Rank-Order for Freedom and Equality
for Four Samples*

	50 POLICEMEN	141 UNEMPLOYED WHITES	28 UNEMPLOYED NEGROES	75 CALVINIST STUDENTS
Freedom	1	3	10	8
Equality	12	9	1	9

midwestern city ranked *freedom* first on the average and *equality* last, showing a value pattern even more extreme than that of college students who were unsympathetic with civil rights demonstrations. Unemployed whites applying for work at a state employment office showed a similar pattern, though not as extreme as that of policemen. Unemployed Negroes showed a reverse value pattern—*freedom* was ranked tenth, and *equality* was ranked first. Finally, students at a Calvinist college showed yet another pattern: they ranked both *freedom* and *equality* relatively low in their hierarchy of terminal values.

All these data on *freedom* and *equality,* as well as other considerations I do not have time to discuss here, point to the presence of a simple, nonetheless comprehensive, two-dimensional model for describing all the major variations among various political orientations. Picture, if you will, the four points of a compass. The north pole represents those groups that place a high value on both *freedom* and *equality,* such as the liberal democrats, socialists, and humanists; the south pole represents those groups that place a low value on both *freedom* and *equality,* such as the fascists, Nazis, and Ku Klux Klan; to the east, on the right, are those groups that place a high value on *freedom* and a low value on *equality,* such as the John Birch Society, conservative Republicans, and followers of Ayn Rand; finally, to the west, on the left, are those groups that place a low value on *freedom* and a high value on *equality,* such as the Stalinist or Mao type of Communism.

Data supporting this model have recently been obtained in a study carried out in collaboration with James Morrison. We selected 25,000-word samples from political writings representing the four poles, and counted the number of times various terminal and instrumental values were mentioned. Samples were taken from socialist writers like Norman Thomas and Erich Fromm, Hitler's *Mein Kampf,* Goldwater's *Conscience of a Conservative,* and Lenin's *Collected Works.* Table 18 shows the results obtained for the two terminal values, *freedom* and *equality.* The socialists mention *freedom* favorably 66 times and *equality* favorably 62 times. For the socialists, *freedom* turned out to rank first and *equality* second in relative

171

Table 18

*Frequency of Mention and Rank-Order of Freedom and Equality
in Writings by Socialists, Hitler, Goldwater, and Lenin*

| | SOCIALISTS | | HITLER | | GOLDWATER | | LENIN | |
	FREQ.*	RANK	FREQ.	RANK	FREQ.	RANK	FREQ.	RANK
Freedom	+66	1	−48	16	+85	1	−47	17
Equality	+62	2	−71	17	−10	16	+88	1

* Number of favorable mentions minus number of unfavorable mentions.

frequence among 17 terminal values. Employing these same 17 terminal values, analysis of Hitler's *Mein Kampf* revealed that *freedom* was ranked 16th and *equality* 17th. In Goldwater's hierarchy of values, *freedom* ranked first and *equality* 16th; and in Lenin's the results were the other way around, *freedom* ranking 17th and *equality* ranking first. All in all, these data seem to fit the two-dimensional model almost perfectly.

Without elaborating further on this model or considering its implications, I want to raise the question of possible inconsistencies within a person's value-attitude system that might involve *freedom* and *equality*. One advantage we gain in asking our subjects to rank-order a set of positive values for importance is that the subject, having little or no awareness of the psychological significance of his responses, has little or no reason to disguise them. In this sense, our value scales function like projective tests. All the values we employ, considered in isolation, are socially desirable ones in our culture and, in the final analysis, the subject has only his own value system to guide him in rank-ordering them. Thus, a subject who ranks *freedom* first and *equality* last (or who ranks, say, *salvation* first and *a comfortable life* second) is not apt to be aware of the possibility that he may be revealing something about himself that others might interpret as antidemocratic or logically inconsistent or, even, as hypocritical. But many of our subjects, upon having their attention drawn to the fact that they ranked *freedom* and *equality* in a highly discrepant manner seemed embarrassed by their ratings. I would

172

suggest that embarrassment is one overt behavioral manifestation of cognitive imbalance.

This discussion of possible inconsistencies lurking below the threshold of awareness brings me back to the matrix of dissonant relations previously discussed and presented in Table 15. I have already suggested that a felt state of inconsistency in relation between two values, or between a value and an attitude, or between one's values and a reference group's values should lead to persistent dissonance effects, which, to alleviate, would require cognitive reorganization. I would now like to report briefly on the results of an experiment designed to explore the effects of such inconsistencies.

Three groups of subjects, Control Group A and Experimental Groups B and C, first filled out an attitude questionnaire concerning equal rights for the Negro, equal rights for other groups, and American policy in Viet Nam. A week later all three groups rank-ordered the 12 terminal values shown in Table 19. Experimental Group B was then presented with information in the form of "Table 1" showing the composite rank orders actually obtained by 444 Michigan State University students for these same 12 values. To arouse feelings of inconsistency between two terminal values the experimenter drew attention to "one of the most interesting findings shown in Table 1" namely, that the students, on the average, ranked *freedom* first and *equality* sixth. "This suggests," the experimenter continued, "that Michigan State students in general are more interested in their own freedom than they are in freedom for other people." The subjects were then invited to compare their own rankings with those shown in "Table 1."

The procedure with the subjects in Experimental Group C was identical with that for Group B except for the fact that they were shown "Table 2" in addition to "Table 1." The purpose of "Table 2" was to induce an additional dissonant relation between a value and an attitude. "Table 2" shows the relationship between civil rights attitude and average rankings of *freedom* and *equality* (the same results shown herein in Table 16). The experimenter discussed these results in some detail and then concluded: "This raises the question as to whether those who are against civil rights

173

are really saying that they care a great deal about *their own* freedom but are indifferent to other people's freedom. Those who are *for* civil rights are perhaps really saying they not only want freedom for themselves, but for other people too." The subjects were then invited to compare the results shown in "Table 2" with their own previously recorded responses to the same civil rights question and their own rankings on *freedom* and *equality*.

Posttests on values and attitudes were administered three weeks later and three to five months later to the two experimental groups and to the control group, which had received no information. The over-all results are shown in Table 19.

Control Group A showed small and generally nonsignificant changes in values three weeks later and three months later. Note that there was a significant change in *freedom* three months later, but that it was in a negative direction. Experimental Group B showed significantly positive increases in *equality* and in *freedom* three weeks later. Three to five months later we still find sizable increases in *equality,* which is significant, and in *freedom,* which is not significant. For Experimental Group C we observe significant positive changes on both *equality* and *freedom* three weeks later as well as three to five months later.

Along with these experimentally induced increases in the importance of *equality* and *freedom* we also observe systematic changes in the rest of the value system. Other social values—*a world at peace* and *national security*—consistently increase in importance, while personal values—*a comfortable life, a meaningful life, maturity, salvation, true friendship,* and *wisdom*—consistently decrease in importance. Many of these changes are statistically significant, and the value changes are evident not only three weeks later but also three to five months later. And the magnitude of change is on the whole greater for Experimental Group C than for Experimental Group B.

Experimental Groups B and C not only showed enduring changes in values but also in attitudes. We observed enduring changes in attitude toward the two most salient issues in contemporary American life—equal rights and Viet Nam. Table 20 displays

174

Table 19

*Mean Changes in Rank-Order of 12 Terminal Values for
Control and Experimental Groups 3 Weeks and 3 Months Later*

		GROUP A	GROUP B	GROUP C
			$N =$	
	3 WKS	47	135	178
	3 MOS	32	93	120
A comfortable life	3 wks	.17	—.48*	—.34
	3 mos	.09	—.57	—.61*
A meaningful life	3 wks	—.23	—.39	—.29
	3 mos	.25	—.44	—.20
A world at peace	3 wks	.34	.61*	.18
	3 mos	.19	.62*	.30
Equality	3 wks	.79	1.47***	1.72***
	3 mos	.44	1.47***	1.68***
Freedom	3 wks	—.47	.78**	.70***
	3 mos	—1.19**	.48	.46*
Maturity	3 wks	—.04	—.10	—.13
	3 mos	1.16	—.10	—.17
National security	3 wks	.36	.41	.55**
	3 mos	.31	.65	.54*
Respect for others	3 wks	.11	.16	—.11
	3 mos	.75	—.03	.33
Respect from others	3 wks	.13	—.09	—.11
	3 mos	.03	—.52	.14
Salvation	3 wks	.15	—.21	—.48**
	3 mos	.09	—.27	—.53*
True friendship	3 wks	—.83*	—1.06***	—1.05***
	3 mos	—.72	—.52*	—1.12***
Wisdom	3 wks	—.55	—.99***	—.61**
	3 mos	—.28	—.72*	—.90**

* $p < .05$. ** $p < .01$. *** $p < .001$, t test for correlated measures.

the nature of the attitude and value changes obtained in four Group C subgroups varying in consistency between a value and an attitude. The first column shows the results for those subjects who had initially ranked *equality* high and, consistent with this value, were pro-civil rights in attitude. This subgroup showed no changes in attitudes toward equal rights or Viet Nam—either three weeks or three months later—and they showed virtually no enduring changes in values. The second column shows the results for those subjects who had initially ranked *equality* high but were nevertheless anti-civil rights in attitude. Three months later their values remained unchanged, but notice what had happened to their attitude toward equal rights for the Negro. Three weeks after the experiment their attitude toward equal rights for the Negro had increased significantly by a mean of 4.57 in the liberal direction; and three to five months later the mean increase had grown to 9.25. The other two attitudes—equal rights for others and Viet Nam—did not change for this group.

The third column shows the results obtained for those subjects whose initial attitude was also inconsistent with their value for *equality*. They had ranked *equality* low but had nevertheless expressed sympathy for civil rights demonstrations. Three weeks and three months after the experimental session they showed sizable and highly significant increases in *equality,* thereby bringing *equality* into alignment with their pro-civil rights atttude, and they also showed significant decreases in two personal values, *a comfortable life* and *true friendship*. This group, already pro-Negro in attitude, became significantly more favorable in their attitude toward equal rights for others and significantly more dovelike in their attitude toward the American presence in Viet Nam. These attitude changes would not have been evident had we tested them only three weeks after the experimental session, but the attitude changes were clearly evident three months afterward—a "sleeper" effect.

Consider, finally, the fourth column which shows the results for those subjects who ranked *equality* low and, consistent with this, were anti-civil rights. Three months later these subjects valued *equality* significantly more and *true friendship* significantly less, but we found no changes in attitudes for this group.

All these results are reasonably in line with the now widely accepted proposition that a necessary condition for change is a state of cognitive inconsistency. We have independently measured this state of inconsistency by asking our subjects at the end of the experi-

Table 20

Mean Changes in Values and Attitudes in Four Group C Subgroups

		RANKS EQUALITY HIGH AND IS		RANKS EQUALITY LOW AND IS	
		PRO-CIVIL RIGHTS	ANTI-CIVIL RIGHTS	PRO-CIVIL RIGHTS	ANTI-CIVIL RIGHTS
		$N=$			
	3 WKS	55	14	70	39
	3 MOS	40	8	49	23
A comfortable	3 wks	.58	−.07	−1.10**	−.36
life	3 mos	.13	.50	−1.41**	−.57
A meaningful	3 wks	−.25	−.50	−.17	−.46
life	3 mos	.28	−.50	−.47	−.35
A world at	3 wks	.44	1.79	−.27	.05
peace	3 mos	.18	1.75	.16	.30
Equality	3 wks	.36	.00	3.16***	1.67***
	3 mos	−.23	−1.13	3.71***	1.65**
Freedom	3 wks	.82**	.29	.80*	.49
	3 mos	.60	−.50	.39	.70
Maturity	3 wks	−.05	.57	.06	−.85
	3 mos	−.48	.63	.02	−.30
National	3 wks	.44	.86	.53	.64
security	3 mos	.20	.50	.73	.74
Respect for	3 wks	−.38	.71*	−.17	.08
others	3 mos	.45	.75	.29	.09
Respect from	3 wks	−.13	.00	−.73*	1.00*
others	3 mos	.68	−.13	−.37	.39
Salvation	3 wks	−.67*	−.14	−.57*	−.15
	3 mos	−.65	.25	−.80	−.04
True	3 wks	−.58	−1.57*	−1.30***	−1.05*
friendship	3 mos	−.33	−1.25	−1.43*	−1.78**
Wisdom	3 wks	−.69	−1.93	.03	−1.15*
	3 mos	−1.00*	−.88	−.86	−.83
Equal rights	3 wks	−.47	4.57*	.09	−1.95
for Negroes	3 mos	.80	9.25**	1.80	−.30
Equal rights	3 wks	−.11	−.43	.20	−2.44
for others	3 mos	.23	2.88	4.33**	−.26
Viet Nam	3 wks	−1.09	.36	.60	−1.59
	3 mos	−.83	.75	1.63*	.74

* $p < .05$. ** $p < .01$. *** $p < .001$, t test for correlated measures.

177

mental session to tell us whether they felt "satisfied" or "dissatisfied" with what they had found out about the way they had ranked the several values. We found that variations in these intervening states of satisfaction-dissatisfaction, as measured, were significantly related to the way the subjects had initially ranked *equality* and *freedom*. In turn, these intervening states of satisfaction-dissatisfaction, assessed at the end of the experimental session, significantly predicted the changes in values that we were to observe three weeks and three to five months after the experimental session.

As I conclude this chapter I become acutely aware of at least a few questions that should be raised about the methods and findings reported here. Do the various value terms have the same meaning for different subjects? What ethical precautions are especially necessary in research on value change? Are the systematic value and attitude changes and the sleeper effects reported here genuine changes or are they artifacts of the experimental situation? Can we expect behavioral changes to follow from such value and attitude changes? Is it just as consistent for a person to move *freedom* down to *equality* as to move *equality* up to *freedom?* Under what conditions will values change to become more consistent with attitudes, and under what conditions will attitudes change to become more consistent with values? Can each of the different kinds of inconsistent relations represented in the matrix be experimentally isolated and their relative effects tested? What are the implications of our formulations and findings for education, therapy, and other areas of human concern that necessarily engage people's values?

I shall forgo further consideration of these questions here since I hope to deal with these issues in a fuller report on a later occasion. Instead I should like to return to the main theme stated in the opening to this chapter, namely, that there are grounds for arguing in favor of a shift of focus away from theories of attitude organization and change toward more comprehensive theories of value organization and change. The empirical findings reported in the latter part of this chapter now embolden me to advocate even more strongly the desirability of such a recentering within the discipline of social psychology.

APPENDIX A

Applications to the Field of Advertising

The advertising man is not the only person who seeks to shape and change other people's beliefs, attitudes, and behavior. There are many kinds of people in our society, professional and nonprofessional, working for pay and for free, who for various combinations of altruistic and selfish reasons are vitally interested in the theory and practice of shaping and changing other people's values, beliefs, attitudes, and behavior. One may point by way of illustration to the psychotherapist, to the teacher, the missionary, the politician, and the lobbyist. All these have in common with the advertising man at least the desire to influence and to persuade others to believe and to act in certain ways they would not otherwise believe and act.

This does not mean that the advertising man wants to change the same sorts of beliefs

179

which, say, the therapist or the politician wants to change. Every human being has many different kinds of beliefs, and every advanced society seems to have encouraged the rise of persuaders who specialize in trying to change some kinds of belief and not other kinds.

What, then, are the different kinds of beliefs that all men hold and what kinds of beliefs does the advertising man wish most to influence? What are the properties of the different kinds of beliefs, and how easily is one kind changed compared with another kind? What special problems arise to plague the advertising man because he specializes in trying to change certain kinds of beliefs and not other kinds; and what can he do about these problems?

Some answers to these questions may be forthcoming by referring to the five kinds of beliefs previously discussed in Chapters One and Two. To reiterate briefly:

Type A beliefs —called primitive beliefs—are all supported by 100 per cent social consensus. Such primitive beliefs are fundamental, taken-for-granted axioms that are not subject to controversy because we believe, and we believe everyone else believes. The data presented in Chapters One and Two suggest that these beliefs are more resistant to change than other types of beliefs, and also that it is extremely upsetting for Type A beliefs to be seriously brought into question.

And then there is a second kind of primitive belief—Type B—which is also extremely resistant to change. Such beliefs do not depend on social support or consensus but instead arise from deep personal experience. Type B beliefs are incontrovertible and we believe them regardless of whether anyone else believes them. Many of these unshakable beliefs are about ourselves and some of these self-conceptions are positive ones—Type B+—and some are negative ones—Type B−. The positive ones represent beliefs about what we are capable of, and the negative ones represent beliefs about what we are afraid of. Some illustrations of Type B+ beliefs may be helpful here. Regardless of what others may think of us, we continue to believe ourselves to be intelligent and rational men, able and competent, basically kind and charitable. Type B+ beliefs represent our positive self-images that guide our aspirations and ambitions to become even better, greater, wiser, and nobler than we already are.

Many of us also have Type B— beliefs—negative self-conceptions—which we cling to primitively regardless of whether others may agree with us. We are often beset by phobias, compulsions, obsessions, neurotic self-doubts and anxieties about self-worth, self-identity, and self-competence. These are the kinds of primitive beliefs we only wish we were rid of, and it is these beliefs that the specialized psychotherapist is often asked to change. Other specialized persuaders are generally not trained or interested in changing Type B— beliefs, but they may be interested in exploiting them without trying to change them.

A third kind of belief—Type C—are authority beliefs, beliefs we all have about which authorities to trust and not to trust. Many facts of physical and social reality have alternative interpretations, are socially controversial, or are not capable of being personally verified or experienced. For these reasons all men need to identify with specific authorities (or reference persons or reference groups) to help them decide what to believe and what not to believe. Is Communism good or bad? Is there a God or isn't there? How do we know the French Revolution actually took place? What about evolution? No man is personally able to ascertain the truth of all such things for himself, so he believes in this or that authority —parents, teachers, religious leaders, scientists—and he is often willing to take authority's word for many things. Thus, we all somehow develop beliefs about which authorities are positive and which are negative, differing from one person to the next, and we look to such authorities for information about what is (and is not) true and beautiful, and good for us.

A fourth kind of belief—Type D—are the beliefs we derive from the authorities we identify with. For example, a devout Catholic has certain beliefs about birth control and divorce because he has taken them over from the authority he believes in. I believe Jupiter has 12 moons not because I have personally seen them but because I trust certain kinds of authorities who have seen them. I am quite prepared to revise my derived belief about Jupiter's moons providing the authorities I trust revise their beliefs. Many people, for example, adhere to a particular religious or political belief system because they identify with a particular authority. Such beliefs can be changed providing the suggestion for change emanates from one's authority, or providing there is a change in one's authority.

Finally, there is a fifth class of beliefs—Type E—inconsequential beliefs. If they are changed, the total system of beliefs is not altered in any significant way. You may believe, for example, that you can get a better shave from one brand of razor blade than another; that a vacation at the beach is more enjoyable than one in the mountains; that Sophia Loren is prettier than Elizabeth Taylor. But, if you can be persuaded to believe the opposite, the change is inconsequential because the rest of your belief system is hardly likely to be affected in any important way.

All these five kinds of beliefs, considered together, are organized into a remarkable piece of architecture which is the total belief system. It has a definable content and a definable structure. And it has a job to do; it serves adaptive functions for the person, in order to maximize his positive self-image and to minimize his negative self-image. Every person has a need to know himself and his world insofar as possible, and a need not to know himself and his world, insofar as necessary. A person's total belief system, with all its five kinds of beliefs, is designed to serve both functions at once.

With these five kinds of beliefs as a frame of reference it is now possible to obtain a somewhat clearer picture of what society's specialized persuaders are trying to do, and which kinds of beliefs they wish most to act upon, to influence, and to change. If we consider first the Type A beliefs that are universally supported by social consensus, it would seem that there are no specialized persuaders whose main business it is to change these kinds of belief. But, as already stated, it would seem to be the business of the professional psychotherapist to change the second kind of primitive belief. The psychotherapists' job is to help us get rid of our negative self-conceptions—Type B— beliefs—and to strengthen our positive self-conceptions—Type B+ beliefs.

Then, there are other specialized persuaders—the political

and religious partisans and ideologists of various persuasion. What sorts of beliefs are they mostly concerned with? Their main focus would seem to be the Type C and Type D beliefs—authority beliefs and derived beliefs.

Consider next the kinds of beliefs that another kind of specialized persuader—the advertising man—tries to form and change. Without in any way denying that the results of advertising may have important economic consequences, it could be suggested from a psychological standpoint that the advertising man has concentrated mainly on forming or changing Type E beliefs—inconsequential beliefs—to the extent that his purpose is to meet the competition, and that he has concentrated mainly on Type D—derived beliefs— to the extent his purpose is to give information. Furthermore, the more competitive the advertising the more it seems to address itself to changing psychologically inconsequential beliefs about the relative merits of one brand over another.

Several implications follow from the preceding analysis. It is tempting to suggest that at least some of the unique characteristics, problems, and embarrassments besetting the advertising industry stem directly or indirectly from its heavy specialization in changing psychologically inconsequential beliefs, and from the additional fact that beliefs that are psychologically inconsequential to the average consumer are highly consequential to all those who need to advertise.

Our findings suggest that inconsequential beliefs are generally easier to change than other kinds of beliefs. This does not mean, however, that the consumer will passively yield to others' efforts to change such beliefs. We generally resist changing *all* our beliefs because we gain comfort in clinging to the familiar and because all our beliefs seem to serve highly important functions for us. So the advertising man, while he has a psychological advantage over other persuaders specializing in changing more central beliefs, still has to find economical ways of changing the less consequential beliefs he specializes in. This he has often tried to do by developing methods for shaking the consumer loose from his belief regarding the virtues of one particular brand over a competitor's in order to make him believe instead that the difference does make a difference. He tries to convince the consumer that there are important benefits to be gained by changing brands, that deeper beliefs and needs will perhaps be better satisfied. The advertising industry has frequently been successful in achieving this aim and, sometimes, miraculously so.

How? The present analysis suggests that the advertiser's goal is often achieved by associating the fifth kind of belief—Type E, the inconsequential beliefs—with other kinds of beliefs tapping psychologically more consequential beliefs and wants. But what other kinds of beliefs are most frequently associated with Type E beliefs?

Theoretically, it is possible to associate the inconsequential beliefs with Type D, or C, or B+, or B−, or A beliefs, but the advertising industry does not use all these combinations with equal frequency. The associations that seem to occur most frequently in competitive advertising are those between Types E and C (the authority beliefs, as in testimonials) and between Types E and B− (as in the old Lifebuoy ads on B.O. or in the more sophisticated Maiden-Form Bra ads that exploit primitive fears of rejection or primitive self-conceptions concerning insufficient femininity).

Why should these two combinations come up more often than the other possible combinations? One may suspect that this is due to the fact that the advertising industry has been heavily influenced by two theories in psychology—behaviorism and psychoanalysis—both having in common an image of man who is fundamentally an irrational creature, helplessly pushed around on the one hand by irrational guilt, anxiety, self-doubt, and other neurotic self-conceptions (B− beliefs) and, on the other hand, helplessly pushed around by external stimuli which, through reward and punishment, condition him to form arbitrary associations. Advertising has borrowed from psychoanalysis its laws of association, and from behaviorism its principles of conditioning; psychoanalysis tells you what to associate with what, and behaviorism tells you how to stamp it in. The inconsequential beliefs have been so often associated with the authority beliefs (Type C) and with the primitive beliefs (Type B−) because the advertising profession has taken over such an irrational image of man from behaviorism and psychoanalysis. In doing so, the advertising industry has come in for a great deal of criticism for a style of advertising that encourages conformity, that is exploitative, debasing, lacking in taste, and insulting to the dignity of man.

Given the facts of our industrial society and, given what Harry C. Groome has in a recent issue of the *Saturday Review* called the *inevitability* of advertising, the advertising man's general strategy of associating the psychologically inconsequential with the consequential is probably the only one open to him and seems psychologically sound in principle. But given also the five kinds of beliefs previously described, it is now possible to at least explore systematically the other possible combinations to see where they might lead us. What would an ad look like which tries to associate an inconsequential belief (Type E) with a primitive belief which we all share (Type A)?

I recall having seen only one example of such an advertisement, a recent advertisement that caught my eye like no advertisement has in many years. This ad appeared in the *New Yorker* (September 7, 1963, p. 138). It was entitled "How to keep water off a duck's back." It shows a duck wearing a superbly tailored raincoat. I might add that children seem to be especially delighted in looking at this picture. Here we see an inconsequential belief about a particular brand of raincoat (*London Fog*) associated with a primitive physical belief about the fundamental nature of a certain animal called a duck. By the process of association our primitive belief about the stark-naked duck is momentarily violated; our sanity is threatened, and it is virtually impossible to turn away from the ad until our primitive belief is somehow reestablished or restored to its original state. In the process the viewer is entertained and *London Fog* gains attention. Whether *London Fog* also gains customers remains to be seen.

In this connection, too, the advertiser's attention may be drawn to the television program *Candid Camera* and to the fact that it often entertains mass audiences by having them watch what happens when there is a momentary disruption of a person's primitive belief about physical and social reality—Type A beliefs, those

185

everyone believes. It is perhaps surprising that the advertising industry has not consciously applied the *Candid Camera* ideas for its own uses. (The *London Fog* ad is the only one I remember seeing that seems to use a similar principle.)

Attention may next be drawn to some psychological considerations that would favor an increasing emphasis in advertising on associations between the inconsequential beliefs (Type E) and the primitive beliefs (Type B+), which refer to the positive conceptions we strive to have of ourselves.

Since the end of World War II, an increasing number of distinguished psychologists have revolted against the image of Irrational Man that behaviorism and classical psychoanalysis have both helped build. Contemporary psychoanalysts talk more and more about the conflict-free sphere of ego functioning; the Gestalt psychologists have emphasized for a long time man's search for meaning, understanding, and organization. Carl Rogers has emphasized the drive for growth and maturity within all individuals; Abraham Maslow has familiarized us with man's drive for self-actualization; Gordon Allport and the existentialists talk about being and becoming. Robert White, Harry F. Harlow, D. E. Berlyne, Leon Festinger, and many others have pointed to the fact that man has a need to know, to understand, and to be competent.

Perhaps the major way in which contemporary psychology differs from the psychology of twenty years ago is that Man is now seen to be not only a *rationalizing* creature but also a *rational* creature—curious, exploratory, and receptive to new ideas. This changing image of man has been represented here by the B+ type of beliefs that exist side-by-side with the B— type within the belief system.

One can discern the barest beginnings of this changing image of man on the part of the advertising industry in certain advertisements, and it may surprise you to learn which advertisement I have in mind: the Pepto-Bismol and Anacin ads. There are probably millions of Americans walking around right now with a conception of a stomach that looks like a hollow dumbell standing on end, and with a conception of a mind composed of split-level compartments.

186

In these ads we see that the advertising man concedes that consumers—at least the ones with stomachaches and headaches—have a need to understand why they have stomachaches or headaches.

At the same time, however, the advertising man is also cynically saying that the consumer is too stupid or too irrational to understand anything well. If we were to learn that our children were being taught such conceptions of stomach or head by their teachers, we would demand that such teachers be immediately fired for incompetence. Why, then, should the advertising man be allowed to exploit, for money, the consumer's legitimate need to understand his stomachaches and headaches?

Is there not a better example of the advertising industry's changing conception of man? Yes, I think there is. David Ogilvy has expressed a more dignified and respectful view of the consumer at a conference on creativity early in 1962; he has expressed this view in his recently published book (1963) and in his advertisements on Puerto Rico, and on travel in the United States and abroad. This dignified image of man is not true of all his famous advertisements. For example, his Schweppes ads and his Rolls Royce ads associate an inconsequential belief with unconscious primitive beliefs concerning snobbish strivings of the self—Type E with Type B—. But his travel ads try to associate psychologically inconsequential beliefs with unconscious primitive beliefs—Type B+—concerning a self that strives to become better-realized, better-rounded, and more open to experience. These ads hold out a dignified promise to let the consumer be and become.

Nevertheless, the irrational image of man still predominates in the advertising world. The more inconsequential the benefits of one brand over a competitor's the more desperately the industry has harangued and nagged and, consequently, irritated its mass audience. It is not easy to convince others that psychologically inconsequential matters are consequential. That the advertising industry attracts such highly talented people, pays them fabulous salaries, and puts them under such terrific pressure can all be attributed to the kinds of beliefs it specializes in changing. It is, consequently, no wonder that the advertising profession is reputed to be among the

187

most guilt-ridden, anxiety-ridden, ulcer-ridden, and death-ridden profession in America.

In closing, therefore, let me emphasize—constructively, I hope—that the advertising man's image of the consumer requires revision in order to bring it more in line not only with the broader and newer image of man outlined here but also with the advertising man's image of himself. To the extent that the advertising man can bring himself to do so, he will gain a new respect from the consumer and in the process gain a renewed respect for himself.

APPENDIX B

Paradoxes of Religious Belief

All organized western religious groups teach their adherents, and those they try to convert, contradictory sets of beliefs. On the one hand, they teach mutual love and respect, the Golden Rule, the love of justice and mercy, and the equality of all men in the eyes of God. On the other hand, they teach (implicitly if not openly) that only *certain* people can be saved—those who believe as they do; that only *certain* people are chosen people; that there is only one real truth —theirs.

Throughout history man, inspired by religious motives, has indeed espoused noble and humanitarian ideals and often behaved accordingly. But he has also committed some of the most horrible crimes and wars in the holy name of religion—the massacre of St. Bartholomew, the Crusades, the Inquisition, the pogroms, and the burnings of witches and heretics. This is the fundamental paradox of religious belief. It is not confined to history. In milder but even more personal forms it exists in our daily lives.

In 1949 Clifford Kirkpatrick, professor of sociology at Indiana University, published some findings on the relationship between religious sentiments and humanitarian attitudes. Professor Kirkpatrick investigated the oft-heard contention that religious feeling fosters humanitarianism; and, conversely, that those without religious training should therefore be less humanitarian. His conclusions were surprising—at least to the followers of organized religion. In group after group—Catholic, Jewish, and the Protestant denominations— he found little correlation at all; but what there was was negative. That is, the devout tended to be *slightly less* humanitarian and had more punitive attitudes toward criminals, delinquents, prostitutes, homosexuals, and those who might seem in need of psychological counseling or psychiatric treatment.

In my own research I have found that, on the average, those who identify themselves as belonging to a religious organization express more intolerance toward racial and ethnic groups (other than their own) than do nonbelievers—or even Communists. These results have been found at Michigan State University, at several New York colleges, and in England (where the Communist results were obtained). Gordon Allport in his book, *The Nature of Prejudice,* describes many of the studies that have come up with similar findings. In a recent paper he read at the Crane Theological School of Tufts University, he said: ". . . on the average, church-goers and professedly religious people have considerably more prejudice than do non-church goers and non-believers" (1959, p. 8). Actually, this conclusion is not quite accurate. While nonbelievers are in fact generally less prejudiced than believers toward racial and ethnic groups, it does not follow that they are more tolerant in every respect. Nonbelievers often betray a bigotry and intellectual arrogance of another kind—intolerance toward those who disagree with them. Allport's conclusion is only valid if by "prejudice" we mean ethnic and religious prejudice.

190

Organized religion also contends that the religious have greater "peace of mind" and mental balance. We have found in our research at Michigan State University—described in my book, *The Open and Closed Mind*—that people with formal religious affiliation are more anxious. Believers, compared with nonbelievers, complain more often of working under great tension, sleeping fitfully, and similar symptoms. On a test designed to measure manifest anxiety, believers generally scored higher than nonbelievers.

If religious affiliation and anxiety go together, is there also a relation between religion and serious mental disturbance? What is the relative frequency of believers and nonbelievers in mental hospitals, compared to the outside? Are the forms and courses of their illnesses different? I recently discussed this with the clinical director of a large mental hospital. He believes without question that religious sentiments prevail in a majority of his patients; further, that religious delusions play a major part in the illnesses of about a third of them.

It is hard to conclude from such observations anything definite about the role religion plays in mental health. This area needs much research, not only within our own culture but also cross-culturally. I am thinking especially of the Soviet Union. What is the relative frequency of mental disease in the Soviet Union as compared with western countries? To what extent could such differences be attributable to differences in religious sentiments? What is the proportion of believers and nonbelievers in Soviet mental hospitals? Many questions could be asked.

In a study in Lansing, Michigan, we found that when you ask a group of Catholics to rank the major Christian denominations in order of their similarity to Catholicism, you generally get the following order: Catholic first, then Episcopalian, Lutheran, Presbyterian, Methodist, and finally Baptist. Ask a group of Baptists to rank the same denominations for similarity, and you get exactly the reverse order: Baptist, Methodist, Presbyterian, Lutheran, Episcopalian, and finally Catholic. When we look at the listings of similarities they seem to make up a kind of color wheel, with each of the six major Christian groups judging all other positions from its

191

own standpoint along the continuum. In reality, all these continua are basically variations of the same theme, with Catholics at one end and Baptists at the other.

Apparently people build up mental maps of which religions are similar to their own, and these mental maps have an important influence on everyday behavior. If a Catholic decides to leave his church and join another, the probability is greatest that he will join the Episcopalian church—next the Lutheran church—and so on down the line. Conversely, a defecting Baptist will more probably join the Methodist church, after that the Presbyterian church, and so on. The other denominations follow the same pattern.

The probability of interfaith marriage increases with the similarity between denominations. When a Catholic marries someone outside his faith, it is more likely to be an Episcopalian, next most likely a Lutheran, and so on.

What of the relation between marital conflicts and interfaith marriages? In general we find that the greater the dissimilarity, the greater the likelihood of conflict both before and after marriage. We determined this by restricting our analysis to couples of whom at least one partner was always Methodist. We interviewed seven or eight all-Methodist couples; then another group in which Methodists had married Presbyterians; then Methodists and Lutherans; and on around. We not only questioned them about their marital conflicts, but also about their premarital conflicts. How long did they "go steady"? (The assumption is that the longer you go steady beyond a certain point, the more likely the conflict.) Did parents object to the marriage? Had they themselves had doubts about it beforehand? Had they ever broken off their engagement? For marital conflict, we asked questions about how often they quarreled, whether they had ever separated (if so, how many times), and whether they had ever contemplated divorce. From the answers we constructed an index of premarital and postmarital conflict.

These findings raise an issue of interest to us all. From the standpoint of mental health, it can be argued that interfaith marriages are undesirable. From the standpoint of democracy, is it desirable to have a society in which everyone marries only within his

192

own sect or denomination? This is a complicated matter and cannot be pursued here. But these findings do suggest that somehow the average person has gotten the idea that religious differences—even minor denominational distinctions within the Christian fold—*do* make a difference; so much difference in fact that interfaith marriages must result in mental unhappiness.

To pull together the various findings: I have mentioned that empirical results show that religious people are on the average less humanitarian, more bigoted, more anxious; also that the greater the religious differences, the greater the likelihood of conflict in marriage. Does a common thread run through these diverse results? What lessons can we learn from them?

It seems to me that these results cannot be accounted for by assuming, as the antireligionists do, that religion is an unqualified force for evil; nor by assuming, as the proreligionists do, that religion is a force only for good. Instead, I believe that these results become more understandable if we assume that there exist simultaneously, within the organized religions of the West, psychologically conflicting moral forces for good *and* evil—teaching brotherhood with the right hand and bigotry with the left, facilitating mental health in some and mental conflict, anxiety, and psychosis in others. I realize that this seems an extreme interpretation; but the research bears it out. Gordon Allport makes a similar point:

> Brotherhood and bigotry are intertwined in all religion. Plenty of pious people are saturated with racial, ethnic, and class prejudice. But at the same time many of the most ardent advocates of racial Justice are religiously motivated (1959, p. 1).

We are taught to make definite distinctions between "we" and "they," between believer and nonbeliever; and sometimes we are urged to act on the basis of these distinctions, for instance in marriage. The category of man that comes to mind when we hear the word "infidel" or "heretic" is essentially a religious one. It is part of our religious heritage. But it is difficult psychologically to love infidels and heretics to the same extent that we love believers.

193

The psychological strain must be very great; and a major result must be guilt and anxiety.

This kind of dichotomy is not confined to religion. Gunnar Myrdal, in *The American Dilemma,* described the conflict between American ideals of democracy and practice of discrimination against minority groups, and the guilt, anxiety, and disorder it spawned. We are familiar in international affairs with the enormous psychological discrepancy between the humanitarian ideals of a classless society advocated by the Marxists and the antihumanitarian methods employed by them for its achievement. No wonder there have been so many defections from the Communist cause in America and Europe! When the strain between one set of beliefs and another set of beliefs—or between belief and practice—becomes too great, one natural response is to turn away from the whole system.

I suspect that such contradictions lead often to defection from religion also. Most of the time, however, the result is psychological conflict, anxiety, and chronic discomfort arising from feelings of guilt. The contradictions in religious teachings are more subtle than those in politics and would, for the most part, be denied consciously. A conflict between ideological content and ideological structure—between *what* is taught and *how* it is taught—must be very subtle. A particular religious institution not only must disseminate a particular religious ideology; it must also perpetuate itself and defend against outside attack. It is this dual purpose of religious institutions, I hypothesize, that leads to the contradiction between the *what* and the *how*. It leads to the paradox of a church disseminating truly religious values to the extent possible, while unwittingly communicating antireligious values to the extent necessary.

Gordon Allport (1959), writing on the relation between religion and bigotry, has suggested two types of religious orientation. He calls them the *extrinsic* and the *intrinsic*. The extrinsic outlook on religion is utilitarian, self-centered, opportunistic, and other-directed. The intrinsic, in contrast, includes basic trust, a compassionate understanding of others so that "dogma is tempered with humility" and, with increasing maturity, "is no longer limited to single segments of self interest." Allport does not imply that everyone is purely either intrinsic or extrinsic; rather, all range somewhere along the continuum from one pole to the other.

The extent to which a particular person has an intrinsic or extrinsic outlook depends largely on the way he is able to resolve the contradictory teachings of his religious group. This in turn depends on the particular quality of his experiences with others, especially with parents in early childhood. A person is more apt to be extrinsically oriented if his early experiences included threat, anxiety, and punishment or if religion was used punitively, as a club to discipline and control him.

Good empirical evidence exists to support Allport's distinctions. W. Cody Wilson (1960) has succeeded in isolating and measuring the extrinsic religious sentiment and in showing that it is closely related to anti-Semitism. Also, one of my collaborators, Dr. C. Gratton Kemp, has isolated two kinds of religiously minded students, all enrolled in one denominational college. One group was open-minded and tolerant, the other group was closed-minded and highly prejudiced. Dr. Kemp studied their value orientations over a six-year period. He found that while they expressed similar values when in college, they diverged sharply six years later. Both groups ranked their religious values highest but then parted abruptly. The open-minded group put social values next and theoretical values third. The closed-minded group also ranked religious values highest, but political values were second in importance for them and economic values third. It is obvious that the total cluster of values is quite different between the two groups. These findings clearly suggest that religious people do indeed differ strongly in their orientations toward life to the extent that their religious outlook is as Allport claims, extrinsic or intrinsic.

All the preceding leads to the following tentative conclusions: the fact that religious people are more likely to express antihumanitarian attitudes, bigotry, and anxiety and the fact that religious similarity and dissimilarity play an important role in marital conflict may both be interpreted as the end result of the emergence of the extrinsic rather than the intrinsic orientation toward religion. They also suggest that, in most people, the extrinsic orientation predominates. This greater prominence of extrinsic attitudes in turn seems to arise out of the contradictory beliefs transmitted through organized religion: humanitarian on one side, antihumanitarian on the other. One constructive suggestion that might be advanced is that ministers, rabbis, and priests should better understand the differences between the *what* and the *how* of belief, and the fact that contradictions between the *what* and the *how* can lead to excessive anxiety, pervasive guilt, and psychic conflict and, therefore, to all sorts of defensive behavior capable of alleviating guilt and conflict. Representatives of organized religion should consequently become more sophisticated about the unwitting contradictions introduced into religious teachings, and try to eliminate them—as the Catholics are doing now with belief in Jewish guilt for the crucifixion.

Parents are really the middlemen between the forces of organized religion and the child. What factors in rearing, in parental attitudes, in discipline techniques, in the quality of reward and punishment are likely to lead to what Allport has called the intrinsic orientation toward religion? What factors lead to the extrinsic? The data suggest that the more the parent encourages the formation and development of extrinsic attitudes toward religion, the more he hinders the growth of the child into a mature and healthy human being. The more he strengthens the intrinsic religious orientation, the more he helps his child grow healthy, mature, tolerant, and happy.

The conflict between the ideal and what seems to be the practical is widespread. But the current readjustment in racial relations, in which clergymen have taken so large a part, for all its upset and pain indicates that these dichotomies are neither eternal nor inevitable. Nor is the extrinsic orientation necessarily the "practical" one. Research and practice in race relations, criminology, and child-rearing have consistently shown that the nonpunitive and accepting approach brings better results.

Change is under way, in the church and in the home, and brings with it, hopefully, greater emphasis on resolving the paradox between the what and the how of religious belief.

196

Acknowledgments

Most of the chapters in *Beliefs, Attitudes, and Values* have been previously published by me. However, for this book they have all undergone varying degrees of revision, elaboration, and editing. I wish to make the following acknowledgments for permission to use my copyrighted materials. Chapter 1, "The Organization and Modification of Beliefs," appeared in *Centennial Review*, 1963, 7, 375–395, under the same title. Chapter 3, "Race and Shared Belief as Factors in Social Choice," was written in collaboration with Louis Mezei and originally appeared under the same title in *Science*, 1966, *151*, 167–172. Chapter 4, "The Principle of Belief Congruence and the Congruity Principle," was written in collaboration with Gilbert Rothman and originally appeared in *Psychological Review*, 1965, *72*, 128–142.

197

Chapter 5, "The Nature of Attitudes," appeared in the *International Encyclopedia of the Social Sciences* (New York: Macmillan, 1968). Chapter 6, "Attitude Change and Behavioral Change," originally appeared in *Public Opinion Quarterly,* 1966–67, *30,* 529–550. Chapter 7, "Organization and Change Within Value-Attitude Systems," originally titled "A Theory of Organization and Change Within Value-Attitude Systems," appears in the *Journal of Social Issues,* 1968. Appendix A, "Some Applications to the Field of Advertising," appeared under the title "Images of the Consumer's Mind on and off Madison Avenue," in *ETC.,* 1964, *21,* 261–273. Appendix B, "Paradoxes of Religious Belief," originally appeared under the same title in *Trans-action,* 1965, *2,* 9–12.

MILTON ROKEACH

Bibliography

ABELSON, R. P., AND ROSENBERG, M. J., "Symbolic Psychologic: A Model of Attitudinal Cognition." *Behavioral Science* 1958, *3*, 1–13.

ADORNO, T. W., FRENKEL-BRUNS-WIK, ELSE, LEVINSON, D. J., AND SANFORD, R. N. *The Authoritarian Personality.* New York: Harper, 1950.

ALLPORT, G. W. "Attitudes." In C. Murchison (Ed.), *A Handbook of Social Psychology.* Worcester, Mass.: Clark University Press, 1935.

ALLPORT, G. W. "Prejudice: A Problem in Psychological and Social Causation." *Journal of Social Issues,* 1950, Supplementary Series No. 4.

ALLPORT, G. W. *The Nature of Prejudice.* Cambridge: Addison-Wesley, 1954.

ALLPORT, G. W. "Religion and Prejudice." *Crane Review,* 1959, *2,* 1–10.

199

ALLPORT, G. W., VERNON, P. E., AND LINDZEY, G. *A Study of Values*. Boston: Houghton Mifflin, 1960.

ANDERSON, C. C., AND CÔTÉ, A. D. J. "Belief Dissonance as a Source of Disaffection between Ethnic Groups." *Journal of Personality and Social Psychology*, 1966, *4*, 447–453.

ASCH, S. E. "Forming Impressions of Personality." *Journal of Abnormal and Social Psychology*, 1946, *41*, 258–290.

ASCH, S. E. *Social Psychology*. New York: Prentice-Hall, 1952.

BLUMER, H. "Attitudes and the Social Act." *Social Problems*, 1955, *3*, 59–64.

BREHM, J. W., AND COHEN, A. R. *Explorations in Cognitive Dissonance*. New York: Wiley, 1962.

BRINK, W., AND HARRIS, L. *The Negro Revolution in America*. New York: Simon and Schuster, 1964.

BROWN, R. "Models of Attitude Change." In *New Directions in Psychology*. New York: Holt, 1962, 1–85.

BRUNSWIK, E. *Systematic and Representative Design of Psychological Experiments*. Berkeley: University of California Press, 1947.

BYRNE, D., AND WONG, T. J. "Racial Prejudice, Interpersonal Attraction, and Assumed Dissimilarity of Attitudes." *Journal of Abnormal and Social Psychology*, 1962, *65*, 246–253.

CAMPBELL, D. T. "Social Attitudes and Other Acquired Behavioral Dispositions." In S. Koch (Ed.), *Psychology: A Study of a Science*. New York: McGraw-Hill, 1963, 94–172.

CARLSON, E. R. "Attitude Change through Modification of Attitude Structure." *Journal of Abnormal and Social Psychology*, 1956, *52*, 256–261.

CHEIN, I. "Behavior Theory and the Behavior of Attitudes: Some Critical Comments." *Psychological Review*, 1948, *55*, 175–188.

COHEN, A. R. *Attitude Change and Social Influence*. New York: Basic Books, 1964.

DEMENT, W., AND KLEITMAN, N. The Relation of Eye Movements during Sleep to Dream Activity: An Objective Method for the Study of Dreaming." *Journal of Experimental Psychology*, 1957, *53*, 339–346.

DEMENT, W., AND WOLPERT, E. A. "The Relation of Eye Movements, Body Motility, and External Stimuli to Dream Content." *Journal of Experimental Psychology*, 1958, *55*, 543–553.

DEUTSCH, M., KRAUSS, R. M., AND ROSENAU, NORA. "Dissonance or Defensiveness?" *Journal of Personality*, 1962, *30*, 16–28.

DOOB, L. W. "The Behavior of Attitudes." *Psychological Review*, 1947, *54*, 135–156.

EAGLY, ALICE. "Involvement as a Determinant of Response to Favorable and Unfavorable Information." *Journal of Personality and Social Psychology*, 1967, 7 (Whole No. 643).

EDWARDS, A. L. *Experimental Design in Psychological Research*. New York: Holt, 1960.

FENICHEL, O. *The Psychoanalytic Theory of Neurosis*. New York: Norton, 1945.

FESTINGER, L. *A Theory of Cognitive Dissonance*. Evanston, Ill.: Row, Peterson, 1957.

FESTINGER, L. "Behavioral Support for Opinion Change." *Public Opinion Quarterly*, 1964, *28*, 404–417.

FISHBEIN, M., AND RAVEN, B. H. "The AB Scales: An Operational Definition of Belief and Attitude." *Human Relations*, 1962, *15*, 35–44.

FISHBEIN, M. "An Investigation of the Relationships between Beliefs about an Object and the Attitude toward that Object." *Human Relations*, 1963, *16*, 233–239.

FISHBEIN, M. "A Behavior Theory Approach to the Relations between Beliefs about an Object and the Attitude toward the Object." In M. Fishbein (Ed.), *Readings in Attitude Theory and Measurement*. New York: Wiley, 1967.

FRENTZEL, JANINA. "Cognitive Consistency and Positive Self-Concept." *Polish Sociological Bulletin*, 1965, *1*, 71–86.

FREUD, S. *Civilization and Its Discontents*. London: Hogarth Press, 1930.

FROMM, E. *Escape from Freedom*. New York: Rinehart, 1941.

HARDING, J., KUTNER, B., PROSHANSKY, H., AND CHEIN, I. "Prejudice and Ethnic Relations." In G. Lindzey (Ed.), *Handbook of Social Psychology*. Reading, Mass.: Addison-Wesley, 1954, 1021–1061.

HEIDER, F. *The Psychology of Interpersonal Relations*. New York: Wiley, 1958.

HILLIARD, A. L. *The Forms of Value*. New York: Columbia University Press, 1950.

HOROWITZ, E. L. " 'Race' Attitudes." In G. Klineberg (Ed.), *Char-*

acteristics of the American Negro. New York: Harper, 1944, 139–247.

HOVLAND, C. I., JANIS, I. L., AND KELLEY, H. H. *Communication and Persuasion.* New Haven: Yale University Press, 1953.

HOVLAND, C. I., *et al. The Order of Presentation in Persuasion.* New Haven: Yale University Press, 1957.

HOVLAND, C. I. "Reconciling Conflicting Results Derived from Experimental and Survey Studies of Attitude Change." *American Psychologist,* 1959, *14,* 8–17.

HUNT, ALICE MCC. "A Study of the Relative Value of Certain Ideals." *Journal of Abnormal and Social Psychology,* 1935, *30,* 222–228.

INSKO, C. A., AND ROBINSON, J. E. "Belief Similarity versus Race as Determinants of Reactions to Negroes by Southern White Adolescents: A Further Test of Rokeach's Theory." *Journal of Personality and Social Psychology,* 1967, *7,* 216–221.

JAMIAS, J. F., AND TROLDAHL, V. C. "Dogmatism, Tradition and General Innovativeness." Unpublished manuscript, 1965.

JANIS, I. L., *et al. Personality and Persuasibility.* New Haven: Yale University Press, 1959.

JASTROW, J. "The Animus of Psychical Research." In Carl Murchison (Ed.), *The Case for and against Psychical Belief.* Worcester, Mass.: Clark University Press, 1927.

JONES, E. E., AND GERARD, H. B. *Foundations of Social Psychology.* New York: Wiley, 1967.

KATZ, D. "The Measurement of Intensity." In H. Cantril (Ed.), *Gauging Public Opinion.* Princeton: Princeton University Press, 1944.

KATZ, D. "The Functional Approach to the Study of Attitudes." *Public Opinion Quarterly,* 1960, *24,* 163–204.

KATZ, D., AND STOTLAND, E. "A Preliminary Statement to a Theory of Attitude Structure and Change." In S. Koch (Ed.), *Psychology: A Study of a Science.* New York: McGraw-Hill, 1959, 423–475.

KELMAN, H. C. "Compliance, Identification, and Internalization: Three Processes of Attitude Change. *Journal of Conflict Resolution,* 1958, *2,* 51–60. (a)

KELMAN, H. C. "Social Influence and Personal Belief: A Theoretical and Experimental Approach to the Study of Behavior Change." Unpublished manuscript, 1958. (b)

KEMP, C. G. "Change in Values in Relation to Open-Closed Systems."

In M. Rokeach, *The Open and Closed Mind*. New York: Basic Books, 1960.

KERLINGER, F. N. "Social Attitudes and Their Criterial Referents: A Structural Theory." *Psychological Review*, 1967, *74*, 110–122.

KIRKPATRICK, C. "Religion and Humanitarianism: A Study of Institutional Implications." *Psychological Monographs*, 1949, *63* (Whole No. 304).

KLUCKHOHN, C. "Values and Value Orientations in the Theory of Action." In T. Parsons and E. A. Shils (Eds.), *Toward a General Theory of Action*. Cambridge: Harvard University Press, 1951.

KLUCKHOHN, FLORENCE R., AND STRODTBECK, F. L. *Variations in Value Orientation*. Evanston, Ill.: Row, Peterson, 1961.

KNUTSON, A. L. *The Individual, Society, and Health Behavior*. New York: Russell Sage Foundation, 1965.

KRECH, D., AND CRUTCHFIELD, R. S. *Theory and Problems of Social Psychology*. New York: McGraw-Hill, 1948.

KRECH, D., CRUTCHFIELD, R., AND BALLACHEY, E. L. *Individual in Society*. New York: McGraw-Hill, 1962.

KUTNER, B., WILKINS, CAROL, AND YARROW, PENNY R. "Verbal Attitudes and Overt Behavior Involving Racial Prejudice." *Journal of Abnormal and Social Psychology*, 1952, *47*, 649–652.

LA PIERE, R. T. "Attitudes vs. Actions." *Social Forces*, 1934, *13*, 230–237.

LASSWELL, II. D. *Psychopathology and Politics*. Chicago: University of Chicago Press, 1930.

LEWIS, HELEN B. "An Approach to Attitude Measurement." *Psychologist's League Journal*, 1938, *2*, 64–65.

LIFTON, R. J. *Thought Reform and the Psychology of Totalism*. New York: Norton, 1961.

LOVEJOY, A. O. "Terminal and Adjectival Values." *Journal of Philosophy*, 1950, *47*, 593–608.

MCDOUGAL, W. *An Introduction to Social Psychology*. Boston: John W. Luce, 1926.

MCGUIRE, W. J. "A Syllogistic Analysis of Cognitive Relationships." In M. J. Rosenberg, *et al.* (Eds.), *Attitude Organization and Change*. New Haven: Yale University Press, 1960.

MCGUIRE, W. J. "Inducing Resistance to Persuasion." In L. Berkowitz (Ed.), *Advances in Experimental Social Psychology*, Vol. 1. New York: Academic Press, 1964.

MALEWSKI, A. "The Influence of Positive and Negative Self-Evaluation on Post-Decisional Dissonance." *Polish Sociological Bulletin,* 1962, *3–4,* 39–49.

MALOF, M., AND LOTT, A. J. "Ethnocentrism and the Acceptance of Negro Support in a Group Pressure Situation." *Journal of Abnormal and Social Psychology,* 1962, *65,* 254–258.

MARTIN, BETTE MARY EVANS. "Ethnic Group and Belief as Determinants of Social Distance." Unpublished Master's thesis, University of Western Ontario, London, Canada, 1964.

MASLOW, A. H. "The Authoritarian Character Structure." *Journal of Social Psychology,* 1943, *18,* 401–411.

MASLOW, A. H. "The Need to Know and the Fear of Knowing." *Journal of General Psychology,* 1963, *68,* 111–125.

MILLER, G. A. "The Magical Number Seven, Plus-or-Minus Two, or Some Limits on Our Capacity for Processing Information." *Psychological Review,* 1956, *63,* 81–97.

MINARD, R. D. "Race Relationships in the Pocahontas Coal Field." *Journal of Social Issues,* 1952, *8,* 29–44.

MORRIS, C. W. *Varieties of Human Value.* Chicago: University of Chicago Press, 1956.

MURRAY, H. A., AND MORGAN, CHRISTIANA D. "A Clinical Study of Sentiments: I." *Genetic Psychology Monographs,* 1945, *32,* 3–149; and "A Clinical Study of Sentiments: II." *Genetic Psychology Monographs,* 1945, *32,* 153–311.

NEWCOMB, T. M. *The Acquaintance Process.* New York: Holt, 1961.

NEWCOMB, T. M., TURNER, R. H., AND CONVERSE, P. E. *Social Psychology.* New York: Holt, 1965.

OGILVY, D. *Confessions of an Adveristing Man.* New York: Atheneum, 1963.

ORNE, M. T. "On the Social Psychology of the Psychological Experiment: With Particular Reference to Demand Characteristics and Their Implications." *American Psychologist,* 1962, *17,* 776–783.

OSGOOD, C. E. "Cognitive Dynamics in the Conduct of Human Affairs." *Public Opinion Quarterly,* 1960, *24,* 341–365.

OSGOOD, C. E., SUCI, G. J., AND TANNEBAUM, P. H. *The Measurement of Meaning.* Urbana: University of Illinois Press, 1957.

OSGOOD, C. E., AND TANNENBAUM, P. H. "The Principle of Congruity in the Prediction of Attitude Change." *Psychological Review,* 1955, *62,* 42–55.

204

PEAK, HELEN. "Attitude and Motivation." In M. R. Jones (Ed.), *Nebraska Symposium on Motivation*. Lincoln, Nebraska: University of Nebraska Press, 1955.

PEPITONE, A. "Some Conceptual and Empirical Problems of Consistency Models." In S. Feldman (Ed.), *Cognitive Consistency*. New York: Academic Press, 1966.

REYHER, J. "Posthypnotic Stimulation of Hypnotically Induced Conflict in Relation to Psychosomatic Reactions and Psychopathology." *Psychosomatic Medicine*, 1961, *23*, 384–391.

REYHER, J. "Hypnosis in Research on Psychopathology." In J. E. Gordon (Ed.), *Handbook of Clinical and Experimental Hypnosis*. New York: The Macmillan Co., 1967.

ROKEACH, M. *The Open and Closed Mind: Investigations into the Nature of Belief Systems and Personality Systems*. New York: Basic Books, 1960. (a)

ROKEACH, M., SMITH, PATRICIA W., AND EVANS, R. I. "Two Kinds of Prejudice or One?" In M. Rokeach, *The Open and Closed Mind*. New York: Basic Books, 1960. (b)

ROKEACH, M. "Belief versus Race as Determinants of Social Distance: Comment on Triandis' Paper." *Journal of Abnormal and Social Psychology*, 1961, *62*, 187–188.

ROKEACH, M. "The Organization and Modification of Beliefs." *Centennial Review*, 1963, *7*, 375–395.

ROKEACH, M. "Images of the Consumer's Mind on and off Madison Avenue." *ETC.*, 1964, *21*, 261–273. (a)

ROKEACH, M. *The Three Christs of Ypsilanti: A Psychological Study*. New York: Knopf, 1964. (b)

ROKEACH, M., AND ROTHMAN, G. "The Principle of Belief Congruence and the Congruity Principle as Models of Cognitive Interaction." *Psychological Review*, 1965, *72*, 128–142.

ROKEACH, M. "Paradoxes of Religious Belief." *Trans-action*, 1965, *2*, 9–12.

ROKEACH, M., AND MEZEL, L. "Race and Shared Belief as Factors in Social Choice." *Science*, 1966, *151*, 167–172.

ROKEACH, M. "Attitude Change and Behavioral Change." *Public Opinion Quarterly*, 1966–67, *30*, 529–550.

ROKEACH, M. "The Nature of Attitudes." In *International Encyclopedia of the Social Sciences*. New York: Macmillan, 1968.

205

ROKEACH, M. "A Theory of Organization and Change in Value-Attitude Systems." *Journal of Social Issues,* 1968, *24,* No. 2.

ROSENBERG, M. J. "Cognitive Structure and Attitudinal Affect." *Journal of Abnormal and Social Psychology,* 1956, *53,* 367–372.

ROSENBERG, M. J. "An Analysis of Affective-Cognitive Consistency." In M. J. Rosenberg, *et al.* (Eds.), *Attitude Organization and Change.* New Haven: Yale University Press, 1960. (a)

ROSENBERG, M. J. "A Structural Theory of Attitude Dynamics." *Public Opinion Quarterly,* 1960, *24,* 319–340. (b)

ROSENBERG, M. J. "When Dissonance Fails: On Eliminating Evaluation Apprehension from Attitude Measurement." *Journal of Personality and Social Psychology,* 1965, *1,* 28–42.

SARNOFF, I., AND KATZ, D. "The Motivational Bases of Attitude Change." *Journal of Abnormal and Social Psychology,* 1954, *49,* 115–124.

SCOTT, W. A. "Cognitive Consistency, Response Reinforcement, and Attitude Change." *Sociometry,* 1959, *22,* 219–229.

SCOTT, W. A. *Values and Organizations.* Chicago: Rand McNally, 1965.

SHEIN, E. H. "The Chinese Indoctrination Program for Prisoners of War." *Psychiatry,* 1956, *18,* 149–172.

SHERIF, CAROLINE W., SHERIF, M., AND NEBERGALL, R. E. *Attitude and Attitude Change.* Philadelphia: Saunders, 1965.

SHERIF, M., AND CANTRIL, H. "The Psychology of 'Attitudes': Part I." *Psychological Review,* 1945, *52,* 295–319. The Psychology of 'Attitudes': Part II." *Psychological Review,* 1946, *53,* 1–24.

SIEGEL, S. *Nonparametric Statistics.* New York: McGraw-Hill, 1956.

SMITH, CAROLE R., WILLIAMS, L., AND WILLIS, R. H. "Race, Sex, and Belief as Determinants of Friendship Acceptance." *Journal of Personality and Social Psychology,* 1967, *5,* 127–137.

SMITH, M. B. "Personal Values as Determinants of a Political Attitude." *Journal of Psychology,* 1949, *28,* 477–486.

SMITH, M. B., BRUNER, J. S., AND WHITE, R. W. *Opinions and Personality.* New York: Wiley, 1956.

SMITH, M. B. "Personal Values in the Study of Lives." In R. W. White (Ed.), *The Study of Lives.* New York: Atherton Press, 1963.

SMITH, M. B. "Attitude Change." In *International Encyclopedia of the Social Sciences.* New York: Macmillan, 1968.

STACHOWIAK, J. G., AND MOSS, C. S. "The Hypnotic Alteration of Social Attitudes." *American Psychologist,* 1963, *18,* 372–373.

STEIN, D. D., HARDYCK, JANE A., AND SMITH, M. B. "Race *and* Belief:

An Open and Shut Case." *Journal of Personality and Social Psychology,* 1965, *1,* 281–289.

STEIN, D. D. "The Influence of Belief Systems on Interpersonal Preference: A Validation Study of Rokeach's Theory of Prejudice." *Psychological Monographs,* 1966, *80* (Whole No. 616).

STOTLAND, E., KATZ, D., AND PATCHEN, M. "The Reduction of Prejudice through the Arousal of Self-Insight." *Journal of Personality,* 1959, *27,* 507–531.

THOMAS, W. I., AND ZNANIECKI, F. *The Polish Peasant in Europe and America.* Boston: Badger, Vol. 1, 1918–20.

THURSTONE, L. L., AND CHAVE, E. J. *The Measurement of Attitude.* Chicago: University of Chicago Press, 1929.

TRIANDIS, H. C. "A Note on Rokeach's Theory of Prejudice." *Journal of Abnormal and Social Psychology,* 1961, *62,* 184–186.

TRIANDIS, H. C., AND DAVIS, E. "Race and Belief as Determinants of Behavioral Intentions." *Journal of Personality and Social Psychology,* 1965, *2,* 715–725.

TROLDAHL, V. C., AND POWELL, F. A. "A Short-Form Dogmatism Scale for Use in Field Studies." *Social Forces,* 1965, *44,* 211–214.

WHITE, R. K. *Value Analysis: The Nature and Use of the Methods.* Glen Gardner, New Jersey: Libertarian Press, 1951.

WHITE, R. W. "Motivation Reconsidered: The Concept of Competence." *Psychological Review,* 1959, *66,* 297–334.

WILLIAMS, R. M. "Values." In *International Encyclopedia of the Social Sciences.* New York: Macmillan, 1968.

WILLIS, R. H., AND BULATAO, R. A. "Belief and Ethnicity as Determinants of Friendship and Marriage Acceptance in the Philippines." *American Psychologist,* 1967, *22,* 539 (Abstract.)

WILSON, W. C. "Extrinsic Religious Values and Prejudice." *Journal of Abnormal and Social Psychology,* 1960, *60,* 286–288.

WISEMAN, R. J., AND REYHER, J. "A Procedure Utilizing Dreams for Deepening the Hypnotic Trance." *American Journal of Clinical Hypnosis,* 1962, *5,* 105–110.

WOODRUFF, A. D., AND DIVESTA, F. J. "The Relationship between Values, Concepts, and Attitudes." *Educational and Psychological Measurement,* 1948, *8,* 645–659.

WRIGHTSMAN, L. S., BAXTER, G. W., JR., AND JACKSON, VIRGINIA W. "Effects of School Desegregation upon Attitudes toward Negroes Held by Southern Junior High School Students." Unpublished manuscript, 1967.

Index

A

ABELSON, R. P., 165

ADORNO, T. W., 66, 110, 117, 129

Advertising: focus on inconsequential beliefs, 183–188; future focus on inconsequential plus primitive beliefs, 186–187

ALLPORT, G. W., 109, 112, 123, 124, 153, 157, 186, 190, 193, 194, 195, 196

ANDERSON, C. C., 64

ASCH, S. E., 18, 80, 87, 112, 126

Assimilation, 91, 99, 103

Attitude(s), 109–132; attitudes-toward-object and attitudes-toward-situation (a) assessment of change in, 148–152, (b) cognitive interaction, 136–138, (c) definitions, 118–119, 135n, 134–135, 159, (d) relation to behavior, 126–129, 163–164; and behavior, 126–129, 134–136; behavior and expressed opinion, relationships, 140–148, 155; and belief, distinction between, 115–116; and contradictory values, 167–168, 168n; definition, 112, 116, 121, 132, 159; differentiated from (a) belief system, 123, (b) delusion, 125, (c) faith, 125, (d) ideology, 123–124, (e) opinion, 125, 139, (f) sentiment, 126, (g) stereotype, 125–126, (h) value, 124–125; functions of, 129–132; as organization

209

211